FIND OUT ABOUT DENZEL . . .

The Child
How life as a minister's son and his mother's decision to get him off the streets and into boarding school finally led him to a career in acting.

The Actor
Rarely does an actor do such meticulous research for his roles, and unlike most, Denzel truly becomes his character with a raw authenticity that continually surprises critics and fans alike. Despite his insistence that hard work alone has brought him success, no one can deny his sheer magnetism on the screen.

The Family Man
Discover how he manages to retain personal privacy in the fishbowl of Hollywood stardom and how his beloved family and faith keep him going.

The Legend
His passion and undisputed gift for acting have sent him to superstardom, forging the way for other black movie stars in white Hollywood. But Denzel Washington is not just a brilliant black actor, he is an immensely talented actor who transcends race-specific casting . . . and is now in a league of his own.

DENZEL WASHINGTON

Chris Nickson

St. Martin's Paperbacks

DENZEL WASHINGTON

Copyright © 1996 by Chris Nickson.

Cover photograph © Gary Moss/Outline Press.

ISBN: 0-312-96043-3

Printed in the United States of America

St. Martin's Paperbacks edition/December 1996

10 9 8 7 6 5 4 3 2 1

To Madeleine Morel, with many, many thanks for her belief.

ACKNOWLEDGMENTS

It's a rare book that exists in a vacuum, and I can't claim quite that rarity for this one. So I'd like to state my indebtedness to a number of interviews with Denzel that have been published, and proved tremendously useful in the writing of this.

In *Ebony*, Lynn Norment's "Denzel Washington Opens Up About Stardom, Family, and Sex Appeal" (October 1995). From the same magazine, "The Glory Days of Denzel Washington" by Laura Randolph (September 1990). In *New York*, Phoebe Hoban's "Days of Glory" (August 13, 1990). Thulani Davis's August 1990 portrait in *American Film*, Elvis Mitchell's "The Mo' Better Denzel" (September 1990) in *California*, Joe Woods's pieces on the making of *Malcolm X* in *Rolling Stone*, Peter Richmond's "Invisible Man" (*GQ*, January 1994), Christopher Farley's "Pride of Place" (*Time*, October 2,

1995), "With Fire" by Lena Williams (*New York Times* magazine, October 25, 1992), and "A League of His Own" by Lloyd Grove in *Vanity Fair*, October 1995.

Beyond that, the thanks extend to individuals. As always, Dave Thompson, for encouragement. To Dennis, the white brother, and to Thom for not being p.c. To my editor, Charles Spicer, for thinking this was a strong idea, and to Katerina Christopoulos, for her invaluable input and attention to the details I missed. Overseas, my mother and father, who are always there, and Mike Murtagh. And, of course, at home, Linda and Graham, whom I love very, very much.

DENZEL
WASHINGTON

INTRODUCTION

Most actors don't have the chance to enjoy an easy life. The vast majority have to constantly struggle to make a living, spending far too much time in unemployment lines, or waiting to audition, and hoping that the next part will be *the* one, that it'll be the lucky break they need to catapult them toward stardom. Almost invariably, it's not.

For African-American actors, it's even harder than that. For many years the roles simply didn't exist, or if they did, they were small, and all too often, demeaning. And, even if they produced brilliant performances, they would frequently go unnoticed.

Sidney Poitier was the first to break through the color barrier, a black man who captured white hearts in a country that was coming to grips with the aftermath of segregation, and starting a new chapter in its racial history.

What followed him wasn't a flow of acting talent, but a trickle. America might have been finally entering the modern age politically, but that didn't mean its emotions had caught up yet.

And that was more or less the way it stayed.

Until Denzel Washington.

Not only has he managed to be taken seriously as an actor, garnering numerous awards for his work, but he's become a bona fide star, one of the very biggest in the movies, a man *Interview* called "*the* leading man in Hollywood for the nineties."

He's crossed every kind of racial barrier; women of all colors swoon over him. Any film with his name above the title is guaranteed a good gross, and to be a hit. And that, in an industry where the bottom line is king, is why he can command ten million dollars for each project. It is also why he could work every single day of the year, if he chose.

For all that, though, as a black man he still has a rough time hailing a cab in New York City.

". . . me with new sneakers on, and a hat, you know, facing uptown?" he told *Vanity Fair*. "Ha ha. Ha ha."

His status as a star doesn't help him on the street. As a black man in America, even the money he makes for a performance can't completely insulate him from the inequalities of real life.

2

Which may be why the man with so many demands on his waking hours has always been more than ready to give back to the African-American community. He's coached Little League, he's been the national spokesman for the Boys and Girls Club for a number of years, and recently he very much put his money where his mouth was, donating one million dollars to Nelson Mandela's Children's Fund—hardly an insignificant amount, by anybody's standards. Then he and his wife, Pauletta Pearson, donated another two and a half million dollars to the building fund of their church, the West Angeles Church of God in Christ.

"We always give, my wife and I—we believe in that," he explained. "We believe in tithing, the church. . . . I've been real blessed, you know, making a lot of money, and you can't take it with you."

He's one of very few actors—of any color—to have made a genuine mark in all three fields—stage, television, and big screen. Nationally, he came to prominence as Dr. Phillip Chandler in the highly praised television series *St. Elsewhere*, but by that time he'd already been making waves, and had won an Obie for his theater work in New York.

He'd already appeared on celluloid, too, but *St. Elsewhere* proved to be the catalyst that projected him toward movie stardom, and the true international fame he now enjoys.

Denzel (the emphasis in pronunciation is on

-ZEL) could have chosen easy roles and traded on his remarkable good looks. Instead he decided to act his way to the top. *Cry Freedom* saw him portraying murdered South African political activist Stephen Biko. In *For Queen and Country*, he was a disaffected British veteran of the Falklands War. *Glory* showed him as a former slave turned Union infantryman during the Civil War. And *Malcolm X* had him as the slain black leader—and it wasn't the first time he'd played him, either; Denzel had been Malcolm in an off-Broadway production of *When the Chickens Come Home to Roost* back in the early eighties, at the start of his career.

He's remained determined to keep pushing himself, never to rest on his laurels. As a major box-office draw, taking the safe route would be a sensible business move. But it would be artistically bankrupt. Which is why he can turn around from the sci-fi shoot-'em-up of *Virtuosity* to take on the role of Easy Rawlins in the much touted *Devil in a Blue Dress*. Onscreen, limits of any kind are not something Denzel Washington acknowledges. He's a black actor, but he doesn't make that the definition of himself. He's an actor, period.

"I don't do films based on what I think people need," he told *Time*. "And I don't consider myself a role model."

Of course, as the leading black actor of his generation, and certainly the most lauded, it's impossible for him to entirely escape being a role model of some sort. As he said, "Color is always important. It's important to me. I don't want to be colorless. I'm an African who lives in America. But in situations where it doesn't matter, it shouldn't."

The stars who've come after him—Wesley Snipes, Lawrence Fishburne, Samuel L. Jackson, among others—all do excellent work, but it's Denzel whose name is golden, the man who's cracked the business enough to have a production deal with TriStar Pictures.

His influence extends far beyond the dollars and cents side of the movie industry. As former Washington, D.C. Mayor Pratt Kelly noted in *Ebony*, "In an era when our youth need positive images more than ever, we are very fortunate to have an actor like Denzel Washington, who has helped to transform some of the stereotypical African-American images we see in Hollywood films."

It's about talent and skill. But there's no denying that his massive popularity has been helped by his devastating looks, although, as author Terry McMillan said, "Unlike many actors, he doesn't let his handsomeness stand in the way of his talent. In fact, the feeling I get about Denzel is that he doesn't want you to pay attention to his looks as much as what he's doing. And that, I think, is where his power lies."

For all that women adore him, and, as he told

Barbara Walters in 1993, ". . . temptation is all around, it's all around, you know, and I haven't been perfect." Yet he's one of the few Hollywood stars today with a lengthy, secure marriage.

He and Pauletta wed in 1983 and have four children, two boys and two girls. She is, as he said to *The New York Times*, ". . . the rock in our marriage . . . she takes on a tremendous amount of weight and pressure. Not only in the home . . . but from the outside, the pressure of being my wife." On a recent tour of South Africa, Archbishop Desmond Tutu led the ceremony where the pair renewed their vows.

The family stands solid and united. Perhaps, though, that's only to be expected from a man who reads *The Daily Word* every morning, and takes the idea of faith very seriously.

Denzel's rise to the fame he now enjoys was slow and gradual, which in the long run might have proved to be the best thing for him. While director Spike Lee felt that, "Where he's at now, he could have been at a long time ago [if he were white]," arguing that the actor was really a victim of racism, Denzel himself noted, more realistically, that, "It's a numbers game. . . . There's a lot of films that white people just may not go see because they see a black face. I think now that they have seen *my* face more. . . . 'Oh, that's the guy that was in the movie with Julia' or 'That's the guy in the Tom Hanks film.' "

From being the guy in other people's movies, he's now indisputably the star of his own, with the ability to draw people to the box office. At forty-one, he's arrived, fully and completely, a superstar in a business where stardom is power, and power is everything. Denzel Washington has become a name that gets projects made, and he's a figure of real international stature.

By now he could probably relax a little, but that's not Denzel's way. It never has been, and it very likely never will be. He's not one to rest on the laurels he's earned. He lives to take chances in his work, because, although he's a star, he's first and foremost a consummate actor, one of the very best around. He lives to act, and act to the very best of his great ability.

But perhaps that's only to be expected from someone whose grounding came in the theater, where each performance is something of a knife-edge, walking a high wire without a net. He's a natural actor, one whose performances aren't full of the quirks and tics that so many feel necessary to put a character across. Rather, he exudes a grace and ease on film, a smoothness, as if he belongs there. His portrayals are no less exacting or three-dimensional, just smoother and more natural, in sync with the small world the movie creates.

However innately talented Denzel may be, though, that degree of skill still requires years of working at the craft, honing, taking everything in, perfecting and processing it for use later. He's become a master of using the small gesture to say a lot—Malcolm X touching his temple with his finger, for example, or Bleek Gilliam stroking his lip.

In many ways, he's transcended color in his appeal. But at the same time, it's always there, to a greater or lesser extent. It's impossible to forget. Which means that in telling the story of Denzel Washington, there are really two tales to be told— that of the man himself, his career and life, and also that of the lot of the black actor, and black man, in America today.

ONE

By the end of 1954, America had become the most prosperous country in the world. Though the police action in Korea still cut close to home, it was a muted sound, and the long blare that had been World War II was fading into memory. The Depression had become something they taught in schools. The goal of a chicken in every pot and two cars in the garage finally seemed like a very real possibility as the suburbs and the freeways blossomed all across the land.

At least, that was the case for white America. If you were black, the outlook wasn't quite so rosy. It was still an era of racism and overt prejudice, of water fountains marked "For Coloreds Only" and riding at the back of the bus. In a land where all men were supposedly equal, the black race had yet to find equality.

The first stirrings were there, but it would take several years for any real change to be effected politically, and far longer than that for the hearts of a country to be altered, if that could ever be done.

In Mount Vernon, just north of the Bronx, and more or less a suburb of New York City, lived the Reverend Denzel Washington, with his wife, Lennis. The Reverend had been born in 1910 in Dillwyn, Virginia, a small town in the center of the state, and had migrated as a young man.

The Church was his calling, but never his living. He and Lennis had one child, a daughter, Lorice, and another on the way. So the Reverend Washington worked two jobs, at the Water Department, and also for S. Klein, the department store.

Mount Vernon, in those days, was a fairly middle-class community. And, far more unusually, it had a multiracial mix that existed in harmony.

"The Bronx started across the street from where I lived," was the way Denzel recalled it during an interview with the *Associated Press*. "It was a good background for someone in my business. My friends were West Indians, blacks, Irish, Italians, so I learned a lot of different cultures."

The family lived well, by local standards. Lennis owned a beauty parlor, and would eventually expand into owning a string of them. Unlike so many others, the Washingtons never had to undergo the constant scrimping and saving to pay bills or find enough to eat.

On December 28, 1954, Lennis gave birth to their second child, a brother for Lorice. It was decided to call him after his father—Denzel Washington.

When they were young, Denzel and Lorice—who would soon be joined by another child, David—didn't see much of their father.

"He was gone when we got up," Denzel recollected in *Vanity Fair*, "and we were asleep when he got home every day."

The Reverend Washington was an extremely busy man. Apart from the pressure of working two jobs, on the go from six A.M. to midnight, which was more than enough for any human being, he also had his calling.

"He was just a very, very spiritual guy," Denzel said. "If there was one person in church and him, they were going to have a full-out service."

That spirit infiltrated the household, too, for the Reverend wouldn't let his children be exposed to the profane films coming out of Hollywood. Instead, he limited them to Biblical epics, movies like *The King of Kings* and *The Ten Commandments*, and the animated Disney features he deemed suitable for kids.

With him gone from the house so much, the day-to-day disciplining of the family fell to Lennis, who was already busy enough herself running the beauty parlors. But though the kids were sensible, it was that added deterrent—"I knew my mother would kill me!"—that kept them out of trouble.

And Denzel, at least, had a place to go that kept him off the streets—the Mt. Vernon Boys' Club, a virtual home away from home throughout his childhood and adolescence, where he could play basketball, talk, or just hang out safely.

By the time he was twelve, Denzel already had a part-time job. Working for your money was a strong part of the ethic in the Washington household; it had been drilled into him, and was something he followed as soon as he could.

He worked in a barbershop, "clean up, hustle, whisk-broom people off, take their clothes to the cleaner's." And if not the most glamorous introduction to the workforce, it was putting some money in his pocket.

When Denzel turned fourteen, though, his entire world changed. His parents, whose marriage had seemed so secure to the boy, divorced.

It rocked him, cut him very deeply. As he told *Parade*, "I rejected everything."

His outlook on life took a one hundred eighty-degree turn. He started running the streets with the bad boys, and, by his own admission, "beating people up in school."

It was more a form of teenage rebellion than anything, not *too* serious; he still avoided real trouble, the confrontations with police that could have left him marked for life.

"My mom's love for me and her desire for me

to do well kept me out. . . ," he said in *The New York Times.* "When it came down to the moment of should I go this way or do that, I'd think about her and say: 'Naahh, let me get myself outta here before I get into trouble.' I think I was more of an actor, even back then."

But if he was an actor, it was purely on an unconscious level. A few more years would pass before he'd discover the joys of the stage.

Lennis Washington continued to worry about her children, that they'd end up growing wilder, out of control, and that was a fate she wasn't willing to tolerate. So she took the unusual step of sending Lorice and Denzel to boarding schools, putting them in places where she knew they'd receive good educations and be well away from the temptations of the streets. It wasn't an easy decision for her, emotionally or financially. The tuition she paid meant there wasn't too much money left over to live on. But in her heart, she knew it was the right thing to do.

Denzel was enrolled in the Oakland Academy, a boys' prep school in upstate New York. It wasn't a place he loved, and during his time there he proved to be no more than an average student. But he did discover that he had a natural ability at music, playing in the band, and also at sports, excelling at almost everything—track, basketball, baseball, and football.

Still, for someone who wasn't good enough for

an athletic scholarship, someone with no real career planned out, it was hardly a preparation for life. So, when Denzel graduated in 1972, and entered Fordham University in the Bronx, he was a little lost. He began as a premed major, only to quickly realize that medicine wasn't for him.

"Not only could I not say the name of one of the courses I had to take—chordaemorphogenesis—but I definitely couldn't pass it," he explained in *California.*

So he switched to journalism. Still he didn't feel comfortable, as if he'd found his niche. And academically, he continued to have the same problems he'd encountered at Oakland Academy, his work never quite good enough. It reached the point where, toward the end of his freshman year, he made the decision to drop out of school for a while, find a job, and figure out exactly what it was he wanted to do with his life.

What he discovered immediately was that the real workaday world held very few charms for him.

"I was just sort of floundering," he said. ". . . I worked at the post office for a while. I worked at the sanitation department, collecting trash. I thought, Whoa! I gotta get back in college!"

But since summer had arrived, instead he found a job as a counselor at a YMCA camp in Lakeville, Connecticut. And there, by pure serendipity, he found his vocation.

It came when he took part in a staff talent show. Although Denzel had never acted before, had never even seen that many actors, both the counselors and campers were struck by his ease and presence on stage.

That one appearance was enough to ignite the flame in him. When he returned to Fordham to begin his sophomore year, he registered to take a theater workshop run by an English and dramatic literature professor, Robinson Stone (a man whose professional experience included playing Joey in the film *Stalag 17*).

Even before class started, Denzel knew that this was what he wanted from his life. To be up there, to become a character, to make people believe. As Stone went around the group of students, asking their goals, Denzel announced that his was to become "the greatest actor in the world."

It seemed like a vain boast for someone who had yet to take part in a real production. But it wasn't long before Stone realized that his pupil just might have the talent to do exactly what he said, even if he still showed no real inclination to the academic side of his studies.

"I had to tell him to get his ass in class 'cause he was cutting so much," Stone said in *Time*.

He became something of a mentor to the youth, casting him as the lead in a campus production of Eugene O'Neill's *The Emperor Jones*.

Denzel's performance left Stone in no doubt; the

young man was a born actor, and he encouraged him to seriously pursue his dream. He went so far as to cast Washington as Shakespeare's Othello when the student was a senior, even though, he felt, "he was much too young for the part."

But Denzel more than rose to the challenge, as Stone told the *Chicago Tribune*. "He was easily the best Othello I had ever seen, and I had seen Paul Robeson play it (Stone had actually acted opposite Robeson in a production of the play). I remember Jose Ferrer came to look at it. He and I agreed that Denzel had a brilliant career ahead of him."

There was one scene in particular that convinced Stone his casting had been perfect.

"Washington was stripped to the waist," he recalled, "and he turned in the direction of Desdemona and crooked his right arm, and as he talked to her his biceps rose, and he said softly, 'Damn her, lewd minx! O, damn her!' Ordinarily, an actor screams that line, but he whispered it. It showed imagination was going on and that he had an ability to understand this very complex character. . . . I dragged several agents to come and see him."

One of those agents provided the kick that changed his life in the biggest possible way. He helped Denzel land his first professional role, a small part as a boyfriend in the television movie *Wilma*, about the Olympic athlete and track star Wilma Rudolph. It aired in 1977, just as Denzel was finally graduating from Fordham—with a double degree, in journalism and drama.

Far more importantly, while he was on the set, he was introduced to a young actress, singer, and pianist who was also part of the cast, playing runner Mae Faggs. Her name was Pauletta Pearson, and Denzel was immediately struck by her.

There was little he could do to follow up on his feelings immediately, though. For he was set to move west, to the American Conservatory Theater in San Francisco where he'd been accepted to study for two years.

Getting into the prestigious school was difficult enough. To have graduated from the program would have assured Denzel of a strong acting career in the theater.

But as his first year progressed, Denzel's interest in school seemed to fade. The lessons in craft and technique seemed to bore him, one of his acting teachers noted. Having absorbed them, he felt he had no need to keep repeating and refining them. Soon he didn't even bother going to class, and just hung out, wearing an Afro and a goatee, and thought about moving on. .

Moving on meant a return to New York, back to auditioning and taking his chances in the theater. But that was what acting meant to Denzel at the time—appearing on a stage, creating a character, and casting a spell over an audience night after night.

It was a good time to make that decision. Normally, a black actor would have had a difficult time finding work—there were very few black roles in plays that were produced, and those tended to be small and menial. But in the late seventies there'd been a proliferation of black theater groups, designed to counter exactly that problem, and give opportunities not only to performers of color, but also to playwrights.

He did make a brief trip to Los Angeles first, to "test the waters," as he put it. But the waters he found there were cold enough to send him back East quickly. And though he spent as much time in the unemployment lines as any other struggling actor, parts did come to him with regularity. He appeared in *The Mighty Gents*, by Richard Wesley, which focused on adults who'd spent their youth in a Newark street gang, Sharon Pollock's *One Tiger to a Hill*, Ntozake Shange's *Spell #7, A Geechee Quick Magic Trance Manual*, and *Dark Old Men*, by Lonnie Elder the third.

There was also a spell of Shakespeare in the Park, where he performed with the Black and Hispanic Acting Ensemble, playing Aediles in their production of *Coriolanus*.

Denzel might not have been a star yet, but at least he was being seen often.

Someone who'd seen him on his return, at a party, was Pauletta Pearson, the woman he'd met on the set of *Wilma*, and who'd made such an impression on him then. Now that he was back to stay, he asked her out, and soon the two were dating regularly. Within a year they were living together—not in some cheap, run-down place, but in Denzel's room in the apartment his mother rented in Mount Vernon, giving the relationship a family seal of approval.

By 1979, a year out of the American Conservatory Theater, Denzel had his biggest break yet. He was offered a featured role in a television movie, an adaptation of Pete Hamill's book, *Flesh and Blood*, playing a street hoodlum who was being groomed for a shot at the world heavyweight boxing title.

It was a very big deal to him. National exposure, a role to sink his teeth into, and a good paycheck. He did what any struggling actor would have done—he jumped at the chance.

For a little while things looked very good. That part, he was sure, would lead to plenty more, so he wouldn't be scuffling from audition to audition, trying to get work, and living hand to mouth every day with Pauletta, counting every single cent to see if he could afford to spend it.

Unfortunately, things didn't turn out the way he'd hoped. The movie aired, but his phone didn't start ringing. If anything, times became tighter than ever. After a few months that brought rejection after rejection, Denzel finally gave up in disgust, and took a job with the county recreation department.

His dream was rapidly fading into thin air.

It was Pauletta who put him back on the right track.

"She was the one who said I should keep going," he said in *Ebony*. "She was the one who said, just keep trying."

And, luckily, he listened to her advice. One week before he was supposed to report for his new job, a role finally came through. Not just any role, but a plum part in an off-Broadway production, playing Malcolm X in *When the Chickens Come Home to Roost*, by Laurence Holder. The drama chronicled a fictional meeting between Malcolm and Elijah Muhammad, the leader of the Nation of Islam. Suddenly Denzel had a big task on his hands.

He knew little about Malcolm X or his work. "I didn't even have a view of Malcolm then," he told *The New York Times* years later. "We just didn't listen to that kind of talk in my father's house."

To prepare for the production, he dyed his hair red, the same color as Malcolm's, listened to tapes of him speaking, and pored through film footage of the man to try and gain a sense of him.

"I remember thinking what it must have felt like to be so free to be able to say anything. It must have made for tension."

What it did make for was a startling portrayal. The play only ran for twelve performances, but they were enough to make Denzel's critical reputation.

In his *New York Times* review, Frank Rich called Denzel's performance, "firm, likable," and "honorable and altruistic without ever becoming a plaster saint."

Word even reached Betty Shabazz, Malcolm's widow, about this young actor portraying her late husband.

"Everyone was saying to me, 'You should go see this kid. He is just absolutely fantastic,'" she recalled. She didn't, because "At the time I couldn't afford emotionally to see it," but Denzel had made a tremendous impact.

And while he was doing his job, the character made a similar impact on him. Somewhere inside, he knew this wouldn't be the only time he'd play Malcolm.

"When I did that play I said to myself, 'I know I'm going to do this movie one day. I *know* it'. . . . I decided then I wasn't going to do anything even dealing with Malcolm X until I did the film about his life."

But that would be a long way off. At the time, being in any sort of feature film, let alone one where he'd be the star, seemed like a pipe dream— a pie in the sky.

But in an actor's world, as he was about to learn, things can change overnight. . . .

TWO

Denzel might have appeared in *When the Chickens Come Home to Roost* only twelve times, but those twelve performances transformed his career. Suddenly, it seemed, his name was known, and there was interest in him. Immediately it led to him working with the Negro Ensemble Company, the famed black acting group that put on plays of depth and resonance in which the main characters were black. But, as he recalled in *American Film*, those were still the great days of black theater in New York.

"It was an exciting time. We were lucky. There were all these black theater folk. We were out there just dealing! . . . We came along at a good time, with different ammunition from the previous generation's. We came along—college educated. We were the first of the bused groups of the sixties and post-sixties era folk. It was just the right combination."

Denzel was cast as Private Melvin Peterson in a new production, *A Soldier's Play*, by Charles Fuller. He was in demand.

"... I remember going from New Federal Theater, doing *When the Chickens Come Home to Roost*, having two weeks off and starting rehearsal on *A Soldier's Play*."

Set on a fictional Army base during World War II, it explored the conflicts between soldiers, black and white. Light entertainment it wasn't, but rich and rewarding it certainly was, and Denzel found himself singled out for plenty of praise from the critics. *Variety* called him "particularly impressive," while *The New York Times* noted that Denzel, "who recently scored as Malcolm X in *When the Chickens Come Home to Roost*, is equally effective here as another, cooler kind of young renegade."

The rave reviews were only the tip of the iceberg, for the play and for Denzel. By the time the theater season was over, *A Soldier's Play* had garnered the Outer Critics Circle Award for best off-Broadway play, and the New York Drama Critics Award for Best American Play (it would go on to win a Pulitzer Prize). And Denzel had been honored with an Obie Award for his performance—no small triumph.

It certainly countered the effect of his first movie. Just before *A Soldier's Play* opened, Denzel's debut on the big screen appeared in theaters. He'd been glad to get the work, there was no doubt about that. Like most actors, he was living on a financial edge, always wondering where the next job would be, how much it would pay, and what it might lead to. The money for a movie was too good to turn down, he and Pauletta agreed. Besides, if he said no, who knew when they might ask again?

So Denzel appeared in *Carbon Copy*. It might have hoped to have some of the sophistication and wit of *Guess Who's Coming to Dinner?*, but in the end proved to be very lightweight stuff indeed, making its racial points with a very heavy, clumsy hand. George Segal starred as a California corporate executive who learned he had an illegitimate, teenage black son (played by Denzel), who wanted to be adopted and acknowledged.

Segal was no Spencer Tracy, Denzel wasn't ready yet to be thought of as a young Sidney Poitier, and the material wasn't that great. Even with Segal's popularity at the time, the film didn't do well—which, in the long run, may have ended up fortunate for Denzel.

But one person who definitely saw *Carbon Copy* was television producer Bruce Paltrow (father of actress Gwyneth Paltrow), who was putting together the cast for a new, offbeat hospital drama to be called *St. Elsewhere*. He knew he wanted a black character for a strong supporting role in the series, but hadn't yet managed to come up with anyone

Solano/Napa Partners
John F. Kennedy Library

4/6/2010   2 47.11 PM

Name: JAMES GLADYS F

ITEMS BORROWED:

1:
Title: Denzel Washington
Item #: 31177014677651
Due Date: 4/27/2010

2:
Title: Denzel Washington   Academy award-wir
Item #: 31177018379817
Due Date: 4/27/2010

------- Please Keep this Slip -------

suitable. Denzel Washington, he thought, might prove to be the perfect choice.

Denzel himself, although he knew the money would be good, had more than a few reservations about committing himself to a television series. He'd already had a couple of offers, and turned them down. But Paltrow, having made his decision, was persuasive.

"I had no idea what *St. Elsewhere* . . . was going to be about," Denzel told *GQ*. "And I wasn't crazy about doing a series, because I thought you'd just get burned out, you'd get too popular. But I was tired of breaking my behind for no money. I went to L.A. thinking, 'This is only going to be for thirteen weeks, anyway.' "

Also, when it came down to it, the character of Dr. Phillip Chandler was simply too good to pass up. He'd be playing an educated black man, a doctor who'd graduated from Yale. It was a chance to do something to break the stereotypical view of blacks that television still generally tended to use.

The agreement that Denzel and Paltrow reached was that Phillip Chandler would be a secondary character on the show, not one of the leads. That would still give Denzel plenty of exposure, he'd be doing something worthwhile, and he'd have the freedom to pursue other projects.

"By being cool, I guess I was lucky. They didn't increase my lines that often, and sometimes I had to paste on a mustache. But it gave me a chance to do all sorts of outside things."

"To be honest," he explained later, "I didn't give a lot of input into my character, because I didn't want it to expand too much. I wanted to remain in the background so I could do movies."

When the series began on NBC, in the fall of 1982, the idea of Denzel having regular movie work was still little more than a dream. There'd been nothing since *Carbon Copy*, and only one other possibility was in the works, a film adaptation of *A Soldier's Play*. So *St. Elsewhere* became his focus for a while. And, to his surprise, it lasted far longer than thirteen weeks.

The critics immediately fell in love with the show, scrambling all over themselves to lavish superlatives on it. Set in St. Elegius, a Boston hospital that had seen better days, *St. Elsewhere* was something different for television in the eighties, a truly adult drama that didn't play down to its audience. Like *Hill Street Blues*, which aired around the same period, it wasn't afraid of tackling difficult issues, throwing in a heavy dose of very human mordant humor, and letting the stew simmer until it became something that closely resembled real hospital life.

The writing was good, the acting superb. The show seemed to herald a new era of "quality" television. And it was rewarded, over the course of its six-year run, with twelve Emmys. But somehow, it never quite managed to catch on fire with the public. Success in the Nielsen ratings consistently evaded it.

Still, to their credit, NBC stuck with the show, and it proved to be a springboard for a number of careers, including Denzel's. The comedian Howie Mandel first became known there. There were kudos in being associated with an acclaimed show, even if it didn't make the "Top Ten."

So, by the time *A Soldier's Play* arrived in theaters as *A Soldier's Story*, Denzel Washinton was one of the few recognizable black faces on television. He might only have been a secondary character on *St. Elsewhere*, but he was a vital part of the ensemble.

That description could have applied equally to *A Soldier's Story*. He didn't head up the cast list, by any means, just part of the excellent ensemble, but Denzel was a very important part of the tale, to a point the crux on which it rested.

Set in Fort Neal, an Army base for black troops outside Tynin, Louisiana, in 1944, the movie was, at its heart, a whodunit. Sergeant Waters (Adolph Caesar) had been killed—shot—on his drunken way back from a bar in town. Reports had been filed, and there had been a cursory investigation. That would change, though, with the arrival of Captain Davenport (Howard E. Rollins, Jr.), a lawyer sent from Washington to discover the truth.

Davenport was the first black officer most of the men, both black draftees and their white leaders, had ever seen. At first tension flared between Davenport and the Colonel commanding the base, and with Captain Taylor, who had originally been assigned to the investigation. Taylor suspected that Waters had been murdered by whites, and knew, if that were the case, that justice would never be done.

Settling in, Davenport began to question the men from the Sergeant's platoon. They'd been a baseball team once, drafted in together from the Negro Leagues, and playing for the entertainment of the troops. But the dynamics of "Sarge's" relationships with his men was odd. He could be a tyrant, and often was, breaking men like Sergeant "Wilkie" Wilcox, who'd become a close friend, down to private for trivial offenses, and taking a rare delight in tormenting C. J. Memphis, his best player, but a slow-witted man who he thought represented the worst aspects of the black race. In his heart, Waters was a vicious man, one who despised his own roots, and who hid his hatred under the veneer of power.

"Sarge" had clashed heads with several of his men, notably Peterson (Denzel), who believed strongly in dignity and found it impossible, after a while, to take the line that Waters was dishing out. It culminated in a fistfight, where Waters, the more experienced, and the one willing to use dirty tricks, thoroughly beat Peterson.

As events unfolded, Davenport learned more about the victim. How, after a shooting, a gun had been found under C. J.'s cot, and "Sarge" had had him arrested, even though his comrades all said he'd been there all night. How "Sarge" had visited C. J. in the stockade and taunted him, until the simple private took the only course out that seemed feasible to him—he committed suicide.

Inevitably, there was a red herring—two white officers admitted beating Waters on the night of his death. But, they insisted, they'd left him at the side of the road—still alive. It would have been impossible for them to have shot him with a .45 anyway, they said; there was a shortage of ammunition. It was only issued to those on guard duty.

That was all Davenport needed to hear. From there he could piece it all together.

He talked to Wilcox again, who admitted he'd planted the gun on C. J. at "Sarge's" instructions.

Now all he had to do was catch the men who'd been on guard duty that night. He already knew who they were.

And they, realizing he was getting close to the truth, had gone AWOL.

Escaping was no easy task, however, and the men, Peterson and Private Smalls, were brought to Davenport. It was Peterson who'd pulled the trigger. He'd seen "Sarge" on the ground, and taken his opportunity. He admitted it, although Smalls had already told the story.

As black troops finally marched out to fight Hitler, and take their rightful place in the war, Davenport left Fort Neal. His work was done.

A Soldier's Story was an important black film. Not only was it a superb drama—playwright Charles Fuller had written the screenplay—but it also showed the tensions between black and white, and black and black. Denzel, as Pauline Kael noted in the *New Yorker*, might have been "the standout," but the movie was a triumph for everyone concerned. Nobody was less than excellent.

Inevitably, it suffered the problems of any stage play brought to the screen. It was static, made up of set pieces, which, for the film, were filled out with flashbacks. But there was no denying the power of the words and emotions it evoked.

It was a risky venture. Films starring blacks, and primarily concerning blacks, were hardly guaranteed box-office smashes. Still, great reviews and word of mouth helped it find an audience, even if that audience wasn't as big as it might have been.

The *New Republic* called Denzel "wiry and passionate," mentioned all the NEC members who reprised their roles in the film, and felt the screen version was "more pungently realized" than the theatrical original. *Newsweek* agreed that "a good deal" of the "crossbreeding of prejudice" had been kept in the movie, but said that "its complexity had been thinned out," and that director Jewison had "nudged the story toward the melodramatic tone of his Oscar-winning 1967 movie *In the Heat of the Night*. . . ."

Whatever the critics thought, suddenly Denzel was a hot property. And something much larger had happened in his life. The year before, in 1983, he and Pauletta had finally married after four years together. She had also given birth to their first child, a son they called John David. Denzel was a husband and a father.

As if that wasn't enough to keep him busy, the film was followed by more work, a television movie, *License to Kill*, about the fallout from a drunk-driving wreck, with Denzel as an assistant district attorney. It wasn't a remarkable piece of work, but it kept his face in front of the public.

And, of course, he was still playing Dr. Phillip Chandler on *St. Elsewhere*. It brought him into peoples' homes on a regular basis. Audiences knew his name from the cast list. He'd stopped being another anonymous black man, another bit player, a token on television, and taken on a real personality.

Offers were coming in, but Denzel was selective. He wanted to be involved in quality work, however much he might desire the paycheck. He had plenty of time to work on other projects, but they had to be stimulating, artistically challenging; they had to engage him.

Which is why, after sorting through endless scripts, he agreed to become involved with *The George McKenna Story*. It was back to television movies again, all too often a barren field. But this was a story worth telling. An important story, for blacks and for America in general.

McKenna was a real person, a teacher who'd become the principal of an inner-city high school (George Washington High, in Los Angeles) that was plagued with gang problems. His goal was to make it a place where students would want to be, and, when there, learn, rather than just waste time. A determined, dedicated man, he did everything in his power to make it happen. Most of his colleagues on the faculty backed him, but a few tried to get him removed. They were, however, unsuccessful, and slowly McKenna did begin to make a difference.

Eventually he gained the respect he needed to effect real change, and the school became exactly what he had hoped. Not only were the students learning, they were winning awards for academic excellence.

As McKenna, Denzel was quietly authoritative, a man of dreams and compassion. For a television movie it was a well-done piece. In a genre where excess tends to be the norm, it never went overboard toward idolizing the man—which would have been all too easy—or becoming maudlin and syrupy at his achievements. For all that, *People* could summon up no enthusiam for the finished product, claiming it was "weighed down by clichéd writing and Cliffs Notes characters," and suggesting that viewers "might play hooky" instead. *Variety*, too, was unimpressed, feeling it moved "too abruptly into unfulfilled scenes," and concluding that "The drama is there but has been parceled out in curious forms." At least the critic was willing to concede that "Washington is splendid as the dedicated educational pro."

Having wrapped up his work on that, Denzel found himself immediately moving on to another project, a small role in Sideny Lumet's film, *Power*. Things were really starting to build for him.

As Arnold Billings, a lobbyist with many connections, including one for Amerabia Oil, Denzel was an enigmatic, somewhat shadowy figure in the film, who pulled political strings. His financial hold on Clair Hastings (Beatrice Strength) had caused her husband, Sam (E. G. Marshall)—an advocate of solar power—to relinquish his seat. In the election to replace him, the Democratic candidate was Jerome Cade (J. T. Walsh), an industrialist. To ensure his election, Billings hired Pete St. John (Richard Gere), an image maker who'd had remarkable success with politicians.

Who he represented didn't bother St. John. He'd walked away from his principles several years before. He did his job for the money, very good money, and he was the best around. But at the same time, Sam Hastings was a very good friend, and St. John wanted to know why he was resigning. He also wanted to know more about the mysterious Billings who had hired him.

He wasn't the only one looking into the Hastings family. St. John's ex-wife, Ellen Freeman (Julie Christie), a journalist, was also digging into the story, and soon she and Pete were comparing notes, only to find they were getting nowhere fast.

Strange things were happening to St. John. His office and hotel phones were bugged. A truck had tried to force him off the road. Something was going very, very wrong.

It was Ellen who uncovered the truth by going through Georgetown property ledgers. Clair Hastings and Arnold Billings had been partners in a proposed office building that literally never got off the ground. Billings had advanced her money, which she had used on her house. With their profit-making scheme getting nowhere, he wanted recompense: He wanted Hastings, whose interests were very different from Billings's oil-rich clients, to resign, so someone more sympathetic could take his place.

Knowing the truth, St. John went to confront Billings, who readily admitted everything. He didn't trust St. John and his questions about Hastings. That was why he'd bugged the phones. And the incident with the truck had been to scare him, to let him know that serious consequences could follow if St. John didn't do his job well.

Pete wasn't standing for that. He quit on the

spot, and went to offer some advice to the college professor who was the third candidate and the underdog on the ballot.

He didn't win, but neither did Cade. In fact, he came in last. There was a measure of justice done, but business would continue as it always had, with only a few minor blips. The only real difference was that St. John had regained some of his humanity.

The movie could have been seen as something quite realistic, a journey through the real Washington, D.C., where favors were traded, market research and advertising meant more than promises, and money talked. Or it could have been seen simply as an exercise in cynicism.

Superbly acted with an outstanding cast, and an awareness of the way things really worked in the corridors of power, the biggest surprise about the movie was that it barely registered at the box office. Gere was a big star, and with the support of people like E. G. Marshall, Julie Christie, and the always wonderful Gene Hackman, *Power* was an exceptional drama.

Given that the movie dealt with the political power system, it was perhaps surprising that Lumet cast a black actor at all. Even in the mideighties, blacks were rarely part of that elite. Indeed, the part that was offered to Denzel—that of a lobbyist for Arab oil interests—had originally been written for a middle-aged white man. But it turned out to be an excellent decision. Denzel showed a marvelously oily, Machiavellian side in the few minutes he enjoyed onscreen, exuding a sense of power and conspiracy. And even when his face was not visible, as Billings he was the one pulling all the strings, the puppeteer behind the whole show. It became an excellent little showcase for another, darker side of Denzel's talent.

The movie might have cast a jaundiced eye on the workings of the American democratic system, and the impact of the money men and image makers on the machinations of government, but in the final instance, *Power* was pummeled by the reviewers, who, oddly enough, couldn't raise much enthusiasm for what they saw on the screen. To them, all the punches it promised to throw were pulled at the final second, leaving it rather impotent. Denzel walked away with some praise for his "ruthless lobbyist," but he turned out to be one of the few involved who did, in a film that *People* categorized as "dumb but entertaining," adding that, at the end, "when Gere finds redemption . . . the only recourse is to stuff popcorn in your ears."

After that it was back to the reality of working on a television series for a while. *St. Elsewhere* had stuttered along for four seasons now, setting quality standards for TV that few other shows could approach, but it was still unable to find a large audience. Only the vociferous appeals of reviewers, endless Emmy nominations (and more than a few awards), plus the pride NBC took in being able to air something so excellent, kept it going. And Denzel stuck with it, keeping Dr. Chandler as a minor ongoing character, staying known and visible.

However it wasn't his work on the series that helped secure his next, and by far his biggest, role to date.

Richard Attenborough had been planning to make *Cry Freedom* for a number of years. He had a script, and he had the contacts in the British film industry to finance it. What he was missing was an actor to play the murdered black South African political activist Steve Biko.

He'd already auditioned a hundred African actors before someone showed him *A Soldier's Story*. Attenborough was immediately impressed by Denzel's work, and a meeting was arranged.

"We had to have a man of charm, of erudition, of intellect, of perception, who was humorous, relaxed, yet confident," was the way Attenborough described his requirements to journalist Hilary de Vries. "Fortunately, we found him in Denzel."

It was, beyond any shadow of a doubt, a plum part, one that had the potential to make Denzel an internationally known figure. He accepted it—it would have been difficult to refuse—but only after a great deal of thought.

Filming in Zimbabwe would leave him shuttling between Africa and America to fulfill his commitments. More than that, it would effectively take him away from his family for a few months, something that gave him great pause. After all, he was a father now, and John David was only three years old. But casting even greater doubt in his mind was the fact that the movie, ostensibly about Biko, instead told the story of a white man, newspaper editor Donald Woods, who had befriended Biko, and who would eventually give the outside world the full details of Steve's arrest and murder in his book, *Biko*.

Attenborough understood and shared Denzel's concerns. But this was the real world. Major studios wanted to make a profit, and a film about a black revolutionary, no matter how well made it was, would not be viable.

As Denzel said to *GQ*, "*Cry Freedom* was disappointing to me because it was supposed to be about Steve Biko. It shouldn't have been compromised by making it Donald Woods's movie. But I think Attenborough knew if he just made a film about a black activist, only three people would come to see it."

But, in the end, *Cry Freedom* offered Denzel the chance to play someone important in the struggle against apartheid, someone the world needed to know about. It was more than just another acting job, it was a social conscience. And that outweighed any of the negatives.

He had six weeks before filming began to prepare himself for the role, listening to tapes of Biko's speeches, interviewing people, both black and white (including Donald Woods), who had known him, reading all he could lay his hands on by or about the man. That alone was a daunting task.

But he also had to physically become Steve Biko, a man not that much like him. A special diet helped him add thirty pounds to his body, making him solid, grounded. He grew a thin goatee, and learned to speak in a South African accent. Then, as the final touch, Denzel had the caps removed from his front teeth, revealing a large gap, all too evident when he grinned. By the time he stepped on the set, he *was* Steve Biko.

THREE

Cry Freedom told the story of Donald Woods, how he came to know Steve Biko, to admire and love him, and after Biko's murder, to write about him and escape with the manuscript to the outside world. But at the heart of it all was Biko himself, which was exactly as it should have been.

For Biko was a martyr, one of many, who wished equality for all people—black and white—in South Africa. Nowadays that hardly seems so revolutionary. But in the mid-seventies, in that country, it was an idea that was quite terrifying to the government.

While the powers-that-be hadn't arrested Biko yet, they had made him a "banned person," which meant that, beyond his immediate family, he could only meet with one person at a time, and his area of movement was very harshly restricted. If he went out, he was followed. His mail and phone calls were monitored. He was branded as a danger to the state.

After writing an article denouncing Biko for black racism, Woods, the editor of a national newspaper (played with surprising effectiveness by Kevin Kline), received an angry visit from a black doctor who wanted him to meet Biko, to hear the truth he'd evidently misunderstood.

Slightly bemused, Woods agreed. He was white, a man of power, wealth, and privilege, but nonetheless a liberal, someone who loved his country, but hated the system where blacks were essentially third-class citizens.

At their first encounter, the two men discovered they liked each other. And that Woods had misjudged Steve. He wanted the black majority to have its rightful power in South Africa, but without the rivers of blood that would follow a revolution. He wanted peace, friendship, a country where black and white could happily coexist.

Their meetings continued. Evading the security police, Biko took Woods to a black township, where he could see firsthand the conditions in which the native Africans lived. And Woods, a white face, was accepted, because he was with Biko, the man who'd become something of a hero for the speeches and writings that had so frightened the government.

And Biko refused to be stifled. Right and justice were on his side. Woods even began to do his part, employing a black reporter and photographer on the newspaper. Woods and his wife, Wendy, came to know Biko, his wife, and children.

Biko spoke at a soccer game, words that were essentially conciliatory. Still, they were enough to have him arrested, through the testimony of paid informants. He appeared in court, eloquently defending his beliefs against lawyers and judges—the men trained to believe in a political system that was slowly dying.

He remained free, or at least out of jail. But the security police hadn't yet had their revenge. Several of them, masked, came in the night to vandalize the community center Biko had started. They were recognized. At his wife's urging, Woods went to see the Minister, Kruger, a man who'd said publicly that he'd accept no corruption in his police force. The facts were laid out, and Kruger affably promised to investigate. Woods returned home, feeling that somehow justice might be done.

It was a false hope, of course. He'd barely arrived home when the police were hammering at his door, demanding to know the name of the witness to the vandalism. Woods refused to tell them, and they threatened him with arrest.

The campaign of harrassment against Donald Woods had only just begun. Police arrived to check the papers of his servant. There were anonymous, abusive phone calls. The blacks he'd employed at the paper were arrested. Mysteriously, in custody, they died.

Biko had the opportunity to address a rally of black students in Cape Town. It meant breaking the law, and traveling outside his allowed zone. Everyone begged him not to go, but his mind was made up. This was too important.

On the way, the car he was driving in was stopped. And Bantu Steve Biko was arrested.

A few months later, still in jail, he was dead.

No autopsy or inquest was allowed.

But Woods was determined that Biko wouldn't be just another victim of the government's conspiracy of silence. He took Steve's widow to the mortuary. Under law, she had the right to see her husband. And when she did, photographs of the body were taken, revealing evidence of the massive physical abuse he'd suffered at the hands of the police. Evidence that Woods would see reached newspapers around the world.

By now the police were watching him very closely. The white man who worked with words had become a threat. As he tried to fly to America, he was stopped. His bags were searched, the photographs of Biko confiscated. Not that it mattered so much. Several sets had already been mailed. But Donald Woods was told formally that he was now a banned person, as well. He could not write for publication—in other words, he no longer had a job.

The pictures of Steve's body raised such a furor around the world that the South African government had no choice but to hold an inquest. Inevitably, it was a whitewash. No blame was attached to the authorities. Biko, it was announced, had brought it on himself, by hunger strike.

For Woods, that injustice was the final straw. With nothing else to fill his time, he sat and began to write about Biko. He'd known the man, had come to know him well. He was a writer, a man with contacts. He would tell the world the truth.

It was a tricky game. His house was under surveillance. It was liable to search at any time. If the manuscript was discovered, Woods would be arrested; there was no question of that. But even that possibility wasn't enough to deter him.

This was something he *had* to do. It went beyond reason or doubt. And, truthfully, Woods had little else to fill his time. The question was, when his book was completed, what could he do with it?

The answer was, smuggle it out of the country. And with it himself, his wife, and his five children.

With the help of friends, an elaborate plan was formulated. Using false papers, disguised as a priest, Woods would make his way to Lesotho, an independent country surrounded by South Africa. Once there, he would call his wife—who had taken the children to visit her mother—and the family would join him. From there they would fly to Botswana, and then to England.

That it was risky was quite obvious. But it was the only chance Woods had. The timing was set for New Year's Eve, when most of the security police would be off duty, celebrating.

For transport, all he could do was hitchhike, and depend on a priest being able to get rides. To make things worse, he had a deadline. He had to be at the British High Commission in Lesotho at 10:00 A.M. on New Year's Day to make the phone call to his wife.

The worst moment came when he was picked up by the police—not arrested, but given a friendly lift that turned into a meandering journey, as the officers responded to calls on their way.

Finally Woods was at the border. According to reports, all he had to do was ford a small stream to freedom. But the reports hadn't disclosed that heavy rains had swollen the stream to a river, one too deep and wide to be crossed. Woods needed to improvise.

As he discovered, his choices were limited—to one. With a ride from a black man glad to be helping his cause, Woods made it to the bridge at the border, and crossed under the eye of the guards. Much later than he'd imagined, he met the friend who was waiting for him, and they tore along the rough roads to town. Time was running out.

Woods was able to call on the stroke of ten. He had political asylum for himself and his family from the British government.

With no difficulty, Wendy Woods was able to take the children to join her husband in Lesotho. Only then did the news of his escape break, and when it did, the South African authorities were up in arms. To reach Botswana from Lesotho, it was necessary to cross South African airspace, and they swore they would force down any plane that carried Woods.

This time it was the Lesotho politicians who came to the rescue. They issued the family United Nations passports, and an official was sent to make the flight with them.

They arrived in Botswana with no problems.

The critics had the same problems with the film as Denzel. It was supposedly Steve Biko's story, but instead, the tale of Donald Woods unfolded. Anti-apartheid activists said similar things, that Attenborough had focused on the white, instead of the black man, the real historical figure.

It was undeniable. But, even so, he'd brought Biko to the screen, and shown the horrifying workings of a system that was slowly creaking to an end. And the movie pulled few punches. It was no apology for the way South Africa had treated its black population.

In style, it was, as *The New York Times* noted, "wildly overblown [and] self-important," taking as its model big epics like David Lean's *Lawrence of Arabia*. Still, *Cry Freedom* was an epic story. From the government massacre of Soweto schoolchildren—seven hundred unarmed youths shot down in cold blood—to Biko addressing a stadium full of people, it gave a real impression of the size and scope of the problems of apartheid, and Steve's popularity.

People derided it as "propagandist," "a movie grenade against apartheid [that] turns out to be made of marshmallow." *Rolling Stone* decided that "*Cry Freedom* leaves little puddles of sincerity wherever it steps . . . the level of naive intentions swells up to your hairline." Or, as *Los Angeles* put it, "the substance is laid on with one of the world's biggest trowels. There's nothing subtle about *Cry Freedom* . . ."

As *New York* was quick to point out, "*Cry Freedom* offers no release, no *danger*. It's a badly compromised film."

What angered most of the critics was the fact that the movie concentrated on Woods, rather than Biko, the real hero of the matter. Simply put, Biko deserved an epic picture like *Cry Freedom*, and Woods didn't.

As the *New Yorker* stated, "Kline probably intends his performance to be self-effacing . . . but he comes across as an unimaginative actor, a void," and the escape of the Woods family, according to *People*, "has no more tension than Julie Andrews and the Von Trapp kids evading the Nazis at the end of *The Sound of Music*."

No one doubted Attenborough's sincerity in making the film. Maybe the biggest question raised was why he needed to spend so much to make it. *Rolling Stone* thought "Perhaps Attenborough needs to learn that you don't always get what you pay for," and *Los Angeles* decided that, in the end, "It drags and stumbles across the many layers of messages it's trying to get across." Pauline Kael, in the *New Yorker*, summed up by admitting, "I am very leery of a moviemaker for whom reaching the widest audience and serving mankind are the same thing."

It didn't win any Oscars (losing out to another "epic," Bertolucci's *The Last Emperor*), but Denzel was nominated for an Academy Award as best supporting actor. That, in itself, was perhaps a slight snub, but there was no reasonable way he could have been nominated for male lead under the rules.

While he didn't win, the praise of the critics filled his ears. *Maclean's* called his performance "charismatic," and the film's "saving grace," while *The New York Times* saw him as simply "magnetic." The actor Dustin Hoffman was so impressed by Denzel's work in the movie that he sent him a note reading, "What grace."

To hear that from someone he looked up to, someone he considered a great actor, was a true compliment. Never mind the critics, the opinion of

. another actor, freely expressed, meant so much to him.

And it was true. Denzel had exhibited remarkable grace in his performance. As Biko, he shone, and made the martyr into an icon for all the world to view. It was certainly more than many people in America would have expected from him. To the majority of the white population in the U.S., he was simply Phillip Chandler. Maybe some had seen him in *A Soldier's Story*, but his fortune—or so it had seemed—was in television. This gave them something else entirely to think about. The movie had broken him out of a mold so many failed to escape.

For Denzel, though, making *Cry Freedom* was more than a career opportunity. For the first time, he had a chance to travel to Africa, which, he said, felt "like a homecoming." This was the land of his ancestors, his history. And, in playing Steve Biko, he was able to contribute something, give something back.

He worked long and hard to take on the mantle of his character, but was never really sure he'd succeeded until the scene where he had to address the football stadium full of people, extras from the local Zimbabwe population. As he finished his lines, the applause that rose was unscripted, loud and honest. As he said to the *Chicago Tribune*, "That's when I felt closest to what I was after."

His portrayal of Biko was, as the critics said, never less than magnificent. It would have been all too easy to glorify the man, to make him into something larger than life, a sainted martyr. But Denzel kept him flesh and blood, and it was all the more powerful for that. You believed in Biko. You had no choice.

With the gap between the front teeth, old clothes, and somewhat scruffy goatee, Denzel wasn't making a sex symbol out of himself or Biko. Women may have started to fall for him from his appearances on *St. Elsewhere*, but this film wasn't designed to increase his appeal in that area. This was about great acting, not pinups.

And great acting was exactly what he gave. To play Biko required showing a great deal of passion—and compassion—overlayed by control, and that was exactly what Denzel projected. He was a man who'd had blows rained upon him by the system, but wasn't about to let it defeat him.

More than anywhere, he showed that in the courtroom scene. Questioned by both the prosecuting lawyer and the judge, Biko answered them as one man to another, an equal, not a subservient black. It wasn't done with insolence, or even anger, but a calm logic that was even more powerful.

Again, when he was talking to the crowd in the football stadium, it was a moment of capturing Biko's essence on film. What he preached wasn't hatred or division, but racial tolerance. And the notes in Denzel's voice, as he spoke the words, held that completely. He *was* Biko.

That was something all the critics happily agreed upon. *People* called his role "powerfully acted," while in *Rolling Stone*, Elvis Mitchell characterized it as an "audacious, intelligent performance [which] provides a mesmerizing center for the story." *Los Angeles* felt he showed "astounding strength," and in *New York*, David Denby rhapsodized over his work, saying that Denzel made Biko "a dazzlingly intelligent man with a special gift of temperament—the ability to argue with an enemy, even contradict him, without insulting his self-esteem," adding that "The softness of his touch draws you into his meaning, forcing you to pursue the mystery of how anyone could be so sure of himself."

The *New Yorker* contended that "every time Biko, in his mustache, goatee, and long sideburns, returns and we hear his pungent, rolling cadences our interest quickens; this man with fire in his eyes commands the screen—Denzel Washington is the star by right of talent," while the *New Republic* capsulized his performance as being offered with "persuasive dignity," and *American Film* allowed that Biko was "marvelously played."

It was unanimous high praise, and nothing more than he deserved. Denzel had said, "The important thing to me was to give people a chance to find out who [Biko] is, and I think we've done that."

But the film also left no doubt that Denzel was an actor who was rapidly going to become a star.

He had the undefinable presence that marked something special from the rest of the pack. When he was onscreen, you looked at *him*, even if he wasn't saying a word. Call it charisma, magic, whatever—he possessed it. There were plenty of other excellent black actors around, many of whom could have done ample justice to the role of Biko. But it's perhaps doubtful whether any of them could have shown such simple strength in the part, and cast such a long shadow to cover the second half of the film, where he never even appeared. More than anything else, those echoes, which resonated until the final credits and then beyond, left no doubts as to what was waiting for Denzel in the future. *Cry Freedom* was an astonishing success for him, a scarcely believable, mature show of talent for someone so young that boded great things for the future. If he could do this, after all, what could his limits be? The future for him as an actor seemed golden. But none of this was going to his head. He knew where his priorities lay. Given a choice between an important interview and going to see his wife take part in a recital, there was no contest. He went to give his support to his wife. That wasn't arrogance; that was love.

Word about his stunning performance leaked out well before the movie arrived in theaters, and offers cascaded in.

But he'd already committed himself to something—not another screen appearance, but a return to his roots in the theater.

The offer had been another that was simply impossible to pass up—a chance to make his first appearance on Broadway. It involved a lot of work, commuting from Los Angeles to New York for rehearsals, then back again to film his part on *St. Elsewhere* and spend some time with his family—an essential, since Pauletta was pregnant with their second child, a daughter they would call Kutia. But the end result, he felt, would be worth it.

Inevitably, when he took on a new role, getting the character involved more than just rehearsals. Denzel wanted to understand, to *know* the man he was supposed to play. With Biko that had involved reading, listening, watching. For his new part, in Ron Milner's play *Checkmates*, it involved getting under the skin of a "buppie"—a black urban professional, in this case a Detroit liquor distributor, a young man who, with his wife, shared a two-story house with an older couple. So Denzel went to work for one for a few weeks, learning a little of the business, and of the people who worked in it.

Perhaps that wasn't quite necessary, but he did it anyway. It gave him a feel for Sylvester Williams, the man he was supposed to be, ambitious, eager, and hiding all his innate sleaziness—homophobia, wife beating—under a superficially charming exterior.

For all his work, though, the play wasn't a success. The cast, which included Ruby Dee and Paul Winfield, two very venerable acting talents, didn't have much to work with. The script had the emptiness of a television situation comedy, or, as *Commonweal* described it, "a reasonably efficient play with a sensible point to make." Still, they made what they could of it, bringing a tremendous amount of talent to the roles. Denzel was singled out by *The Village Voice* as an actor who "animates the most repugnant (and confusingly written) of the four characters with a likability, vocal precision, and free-flowing body language that makes me want to see him in Shakespeare or as the wolfish hero of some Restoration comedy," while *Commonweal* curtly labeled his characterization as "essentially likable."

The box office for the play did enjoy a small boost when a little controversy surrounded its opening. In an interview with *The New York Times*, Denzel described it as "theater whose players happen to be black," prompting a reply in the newspaper from playwright Milner, who had, as *Commonweal* said, "long insisted that black playwrights should write black plays for black audiences," and who announced that Denzel had misheard him. Not that the tempest in a teacup generated too much electricity or interest: *Checkmates* still didn't enjoy a long run. It did, however, mean that Denzel had now achieved the Broadway goal of every stage actor. Having conquered that peak, it was time to look back to the movies, and this time, a starring role.

Unfortunately, it was in a British film that barely made it to the screens in America, leaving a remarkably strong performance to vanish, virtually unnoticed.

With a working-class English accent firmly (and as convincing as the South African accent he'd mastered for Biko) in place, Denzel starred as Ruben, an Afro-Caribbean man home from fighting in the Falklands, where the British had defeated Argentina in the early eighties.

In the Army he'd known where he stood. He'd fought for something, achieved something. But at home again, he began to realize that the ideals that had stood in his mind were all false.

The police, far from being the protectors of the innocent, took every opportunity to pick on blacks. All around Ruben, the tension was building, in a state where the gulf between the haves and have-nots was visibly widening every day.

Ruben found himself torn between loyalty to the system he'd served, which up close reeked of corruption, and which was rapidly falling apart, or to his friends, like Fish, with whom he'd been in the service, and who now was crippled, and cast on the scrap heap by the State, or Stacey, Ruben's white girlfriend. Even Colin, who'd gone on to become one of the haves in this new society, had only managed to escape the slums by dealing drugs.

The final result, inevitably, was tragedy, and Ruben learned that the system was too powerful. No one man could overcome it. Even a group stood next to no chance, particularly when that group was black, and essentially disenfranchised.

For Queen and Country was a sharp indictment of the country that England had become, where the concept of justice for all had been lost in the rampant greed stimulated by the Thatcher government, a time when individual rights meant a lot less than a bulging bank account. Power was might, and Ruben, quite simply, had no power.

As Denzel said later, ". . . that was a bleak film. The subject matter was tough, the kind of movie that wouldn't get made in this country; a movie about the dilemma of the black veteran."

The *New Leader* called it "an urban melodrama set in the housing estates of southeast London [which] not only moves its characters toward defeat, it starts them off that way." And, truly, the film was suffused with an atmosphere of despondency and decay. While the critic, John Morrone, praised Denzel, who "brings more quiet strength than he can actually use" to the role of Ruben, he also mentioned the "uncommonly well-conceived ensemble of supporting roles."

All in all, it was powerful stuff, and, after Denzel's marvelous portrayal of Steve Biko, it was interesting to see him play someone who was, essentially, the other side of the coin: powerless and stifled. But, more than anything, it affirmed what an actor he'd become, able to take on and master anything, and never offer less than a superb performance. Maybe the greatest loss was that the movie was never given a chance to make an impact in America, largely because the company that was supposed to distribute it went bankrupt, and no one else picked it up.

FOUR

By 1989, though, an outsider could have been forgiven for thinking that Denzel was forging a movie career as a character actor. He was starring in films now, but not as an American, or as someone he could immediately relate to. First had been Biko, then Ruben. So that feeling was only heightened when he appeared in *The Mighty Quinn*, playing the title role of Xavier Quinn, the police chief on a small, unnamed Caribbean island.

Why was he chosen? *Cry Freedom* had received excellent reviews, and Denzel's Oscar nomination for best supporting actor had given him some name recognition and made him a relatively bankable quantity. *For Queen and Country*, although not widely seen, showed that his onscreen power continued to grow. Having Denzel involved in the project was a guarantee there'd be good acting. He brought some style to the concept.

Why did he accept? It was another starring role, something to establish him at that level. Also, quite possibly it was better than many of the other roles being offered to him, giving him a chance to expand his range a little more.

On top of that, the movie did have a certain appeal. For the first time, it gave him the chance to play a heroic figure on the side of law and order, the black man as the crime fighter, rather than the criminal, as he was becoming stereotyped by society.

Xavier Quinn had grown up on the island. While his childhood best friend, Maubee (a dreadlocked Robert Townsend, looking and sounding very convincing) had drifted into petty crime and free living and loving, Quinn had made something of his life. After three years in the U.S. Marines, he'd gone to the FBI school at Quantico, coming home with ample qualifications to be the chief of police, a position he enjoyed, although recently his work, and the change it had caused in him, had brought about a separation between him and his wife.

Not that the island had too much crime. At least, until a rich white man, Walter Pater, was found dead at the resort he owned, his throat cut, the body lying, and boiling, in a Jacuzzi.

As Quinn raced up the mountain road to the

crime scene, he almost had an accident with Maubee, who was driving down recklessly on his motorcycle with his girlfriend Isola in the sidecar. The suitcase she'd been carrying landed in the road between them. Maubee took it back.

A visiting doctor had already examined Pater's body, and was certain the slit throat was the cause of death. Quinn, though, wanted to play this by the book, ordering the corpse to be taken for an autopsy.

Elgin (James Fox), the resort manager, resented Quinn's interference. He was already convinced that Maubee was guilty of the crime. And, when Quinn saw that the dead man's luggage matched the case Maubee had been carrying on his bike, it certainly seemed possible that his old friend was involved. But murder? There was no way he could believe that. Maubee would do a lot of things—indeed, he had almost a Robin Hood reputation on the island—but he wouldn't kill a man.

Still, it looked bad when Maubee was almost caught by the police, just escaping from a bar, after betting a man ten thousand U.S. dollars that he couldn't drink a glass of beer and ganja butts. He'd seen the note, the man insisted—it was a ten thousand dollar bill. But no such denomination existed.

Quinn began to find himself in a situation that was as much political as criminal. His boss, the island's governor, wanted Maubee arrested for the crime. At the same time, he wouldn't allow Quinn to conduct an autopsy. It was unnecessary, he said; the cause of death was already known. The body was already at the airport, waiting to be shipped home.

But Quinn wasn't going to allow anything like official disapproval deter him from his investigation, though. In the middle of the night he took the coroner to the airport hangar, where the real truth was discovered—Pater had died from a snakebite.

Now Quinn needed to find Maubee, to stop him from being railroaded for a crime he hadn't committed. But his job was becoming harder. On the governer's orders, he was now accompanied by an American, Miller, an "employee" of Pater's, assigned to tie up all the loose ends.

They visited Isola's aunt, trying to find information, but the old lady, a witch, offered none. Quinn was stymied.

It got worse. Finding himself followed by an unknown man in a green Volkswagen, he stopped, and searched the man, only to discover he was carrying a pistol and silencer. Quinn arrested him, but as soon as he made his phone call, he was released—on the governer's orders. What was going on here?

The answer was more simple, and at the same time more complex, than anyone could have realized. Pater was the conduit between the U.S. government and some South American rebels. The suitcase Maubee had taken contained money meant for the rebels. But, with Pater's death, the operation had been canceled. The large American had come down to retrieve the cash. The gunman, a courier for the rebels, was also there to pick it up.

The game grew more dangerous when the gunman was found dead in his hotel room, shot in the head by Miller, who also returned to Isola's aunt, and killed her trying to discover Maubee's whereabouts.

Finally Isola told Quinn where Maubee was hiding, and he went there. He knew some of the truth, and had guessed the rest. Ten thousand dollar bills did exist, although they hadn't been in circulation for decades.

Maubee supplied the missing pieces of the puzzle. Isola had worked at the resort, and become pregnant by Pater, who'd fired her from her job there. Seeking retribution, she'd taken a snake to his room there, and it had killed him. To diguise that, Maubee had cut the corpse's throat, and put him in the Jacuzzi. Then, seeing the open suitcase of money, he'd taken it. After that everything had gotten out of hand.

But it wasn't over yet. The American had followed Quinn in a helicopter. He was armed, and extremely dangerous. He wanted the money, and Maubee was willing to pass it over. Quinn, without his gun, was powerless to stop it all from happening.

The helicopter lifted off. The American had his

money, now in a sack. It was impossible to say why, but Maubee was hanging onto one of the skids. The American fired at him, and he fell.

In death, though, Maubee had his final revenge. The sack contained a snake. Slithering out, it bit the pilot, and the helicopter crashed in a ball of flame.

Quinn was shattered. His best friend was dead— too many people were dead over a bag of money. His authority had been shown to be a sham. The world had changed around him.

Dispirited, he returned to his wife. She took him in.

But was Maubee really dead? Footprints in the sand, leading to a place where a ten-thousand-dollar bill wedged between two rocks, left one wondering . . .

Still, that was for a sequel, although one was never made. It was the era of sequels and prequels in Hollywood, but *The Mighty Quinn* wasn't successful enough to warrant one. The critics enjoyed the movie, but audiences didn't fill the theaters to see it.

In truth, it was a case of having actors who outstripped their material. The film was entertaining enough, and captured the relaxed ambience of the islands (helped by a strong reggae sound track), but the story, however much it tried, couldn't pack a big enough punch. The plot was too convoluted, and the main characters weren't developed as much as they could have been.

New York felt that the actors "Away from America . . . seem to be having an unconstrained good time." But the magazine wondered why it was necessary to interrupt the plot with musical numbers, a question echoed by *Variety*, who felt they "destroy the narrative flow."

In fact *Variety* found little worthwhile in the film at all, dismissing the script as "pointless," the direction as "overly flashy," and the cast as "barely adequate," and the "decision to use mainly American thesp[ian]s fitted with variable West Indian accents destroys credibility."

People, too, had problems with the "scattershot" script, and even *Library Journal* admitted that "The grand finale reveals a twist more complicated than the lackadaisical story really warrants."

But for everyone the big news here was Denzel. While all the critics agreed that this was not a star-making performance for him, they realized it was just a matter of time before he became a major figure in American movies. As David Denby wrote in *New York*, "He has a quick, fluid intelligence, fierce concentration, a beautiful voice, and a graceful way of taking the obvious macho emphasis out of an action role," concluding that "sooner or later, Denzel Washington will become a great movie star." *People* decided that he "wields a leading man's charm and confidence. . . . He gives a small-time film some big-time appeal," and began the review with a fairly definitive sentence: "When Denzel

Washington finally achieves major film-star status, this quirky thriller will serve as a historical footnote to his career."

It seemed as if the reviewers were in agreement. This wasn't a great film, by any means (although *Library Journal* conceded that it was "enjoyable . . . if not entirely satisfying") but it gave a strong indication of Denzel's screen charisma. Stardom was coming. That was inevitable. The only questions remaining were how and when it would happen.

The Mighty Quinn did one other thing for Denzel. For the first time, it allowed him to play a character with a romantic life. Admittedly, not the best one, but, as he said himself, "Rarely do we get to see blacks in romantic parts."

And Sheryl Lee Ralph, who played Lola, his wife, expanded on that. "I like the fact that Denzel's character and mine share a relationship that we have not seen on the screen . . . a black couple that's healthy, together, and trying to work it out. Nobody's kicking anybody's butt, nobody's hooking or pimping or whatever. We're a wholesome couple having some problems that we're trying to work out."

Which was true. It did make a refreshing change from the way blacks were usually portrayed in movies. And in that regard, *The Mighty Quinn* was a big step forward.

It certainly was for Denzel. A starring role in a movie that received wide distribution in America, even if it wasn't a box-office success, proved that he was on his way, that his climb to the top was simply a matter of time.

For now, though, he was moving on to something very different, to another time and place, and something of great black historical significance.

FIVE

It could have been seen as a move backward for Denzel to take a supporting part after starring, or co-starring, roles. And, in many cases, that would have been true. But when the film was something special, indeed something quite remarkable, like *Glory*, then the gradations of stardom became far less important to him.

One of the lesser known facts of the Civil War is that one hundred and eighty thousand black troops fought on the Union side. Certainly, Denzel himself didn't know it before he was offered the script. But they had an important place in Lincoln's victory, and this film intended to tell a small part of that story.

The first of the black units was the 54th Regiment of the Massachusetts Voluntary Infantry, raised in Boston from free men and escaped slaves, all of whom believed in their cause with a fervor that went far beyond their white counterparts.

The man at the head of this regiment was ridiculously young for his rank. Robert Gould Shaw (Matthew Broderick) was twenty-three. He'd been wounded at the battle of Antietam, leading his men in a charge, and was recuperating at his parents' home when the proposition was put to him—the chance to lead his own regiment, the first colored regiment.

At first he was unsure. The death and decay he'd seen on the battlefield scared him, and left him with the knowledge that war was nothing glorious, even for the best of causes.

But he agreed, and asked his best friend, somewhat of a fop and drunkard, to join him. Before he'd taken three steps, he had his first volunteer— Thomas, a free black man, and an educated, literary man, who was overjoyed to be given the chance to fight against slavery.

The ranks quickly swelled, and it wasn't long before Shaw had his volunteers. They were a raggletaggle bunch, mostly uneducated former slaves who'd escaped from the South, and who saw this as their chance to bring down a system that had treated them as something less than human.

Shaw and his band went to camp, where they'd all be trained, and learn about life in slightly different ways. Thomas found himself sharing a tent with men less educated than himself, whose pasts

were very different. There was Trip (Denzel), the
angry ex-slave who'd escaped when he was twelve.
And the simple but eager country boy, who asked
Thomas to teach him to read. Then the older man
(Morgan Freeman), calmer and wiser, who seemed
capable of easing the tensions between his tentmates. Under the stern eye and harsh words of the
drill sergeant, Mulcahy, they, and the other troops,
began to take on some sort of order and discipline,
to think like soldiers. And, isolated by his command, Shaw began to grow fully into his manhood.

Official word reached him that the South had announced that any black caught on the battlefield
would be returned to slavery. If that man was in a
Union uniform, he would be executed. The same
applied to white officers leading blacks. He read
the proclamation to his men, telling them that any
man wishing to leave would be honorably dis-
charged.

The next morning, at parade, they were all still
there, more determined than ever.

Shaw was already fighting battles, not against
the Confederacy, but against a more nebulous enemy—an army bureaucracy that refused to take
Negro soldiers seriously. His men needed guns,
shoes, and uniforms, but he was frustrated in his
attempts to get them.

Rifles, however, did finally arrive, and the men
were trained to shoot and use bayonets. But still no
boots or uniforms. The men wanted to fight, but it

seemed they'd never have their chance.

Then Trip, always rebellious, was caught trying to leave camp. Shaw had no alternative. Under regulations, the man had to be flogged in front of everyone. Just like a slave. During the whipping, Trip was completely silent, merely looking at Shaw in dumb accusation.

He'd gone to try to find a pair of boots. The men were exhausting themselves every day, then going back to their tents with feet swollen and bloody in their cheap shoes.

Finally Shaw took some of his men and used his rank to bully the Quartermaster into giving him boots and socks for his soldiers. Maybe it wasn't much, but it meant a lot.

However, at every turn, things seemed to conspire against him. When the troops were due to be paid, he had to read an order stating that Negro troops were to be paid less than whites. Under Trip's incitement, the regiment came close to mutiny, tearing up their paysheets, refusing to be treated as lesser men. Shaw restored order by saying, in solidarity, that if his men wouldn't draw their pay, no one in the regiment would. At that point the bond between commander and men became solid.

Then the uniforms arrived. His people were trained, and now they looked like soldiers. The 54th was ready to do its part. After a march through Boston, they headed South, to the enemy.

But the South Carolina where they landed held no Confederate troops—they were long gone. Instead they found slaves, plantations untroubled by war, humming along to the rhythm of long days with no prospect of fighting.

Shaw and his men came under the command of Colonel Montgomery, a Southerner who led the only other black regiment, raised from freed slaves. Compared to the 54th, they were little more than rabble, and Montgomery treated them that way, as if he were still in his native Kentucky, and they were his property. He had both regiments move into Georgia and destroy a small town, a place where only civilians lived, to teach the secessionists a lesson.

Of course, all it achieved was to set white minds more firmly against the blacks who came and set fire to their houses.

The 54th became nothing more than a work detail, which wasn't what any of them had signed up for. They'd joined to fight, and they were being denied the chance—all because the men were black.

Eventually Shaw reluctantly resorted to blackmail. If his commanding officer did not reassign the men to the line, he'd have no choice but to write to certain people in Washington—and, since his father was a prominent abolitionist, Shaw would be listened to—about irregularities of looting and altered bookkeeping that had been going on.

The commander surrendered without a fight.

All too soon the 54th saw their first real blood, standing up to a line of cavalry, then an infantry charge, which they repelled in grand fashion. Men died, but now they were fighting, doing the job they'd wanted, that they'd trained so hard to do.

What they really wanted was glory.

And their chance would come soon enough.

General Strong took his officers along the beach to show them Fort Wagner, where the Confederates had a stronghold. It needed to be taken, and there was only one approach route the army could take, a killing floor. He needed a regiment to volunteer to be the first through, to soak up the extreme casualties that would be inevitable in such an assault, but who might soften up the defenses enough for those following to take the place.

Shaw offered the 54th.

It was suicide, and he knew it. But it was his chance to show the faith he had in his men, in their ability and desire to take part in this war.

The troops, too, knew the odds against them, but no man backed down. Next morning they marched proudly from camp, to the cheers of their colleagues.

They assembled on the beach. The drummer boys were sent to the rear.

The charge began slowly, at walking pace, then accelerated to double time. The artillery had them pinpointed on the sand, and shells kept thinning the ranks.

But they made the outer wall. The standard bearer fell, and Trip, who'd earlier refused the job, lifted the Colors. They moved on, overcoming a wave of defenders, losing men all the time. Shaw went down, then Trip, and Thomas.

And that was as far as they could ever get. The forces inside the Fort were simply too large to over-power.

In that one attack, the 54th lost over half its men. The fort was never taken. The men had their glory, but all it left them with was death, a single grave by the shore where they were all tumbled together, black and white.

Denzel had had one problem about being involved with the film. He was, he said, "very hesitant about doing quote unquote slave films, but the bottom line is that as a black American, that's my history, and this isn't [a slave film]."

It certainly wasn't. If anything, it was about free men making their choices. And if the central character was white—Shaw and the 54th had actually existed—the black soldiers still played a very important part in the movie.

Given its very noble aims, it was perhaps a shame that the film ended up being somewhat overblown, and occasionally melodramatic. It wanted desperately to be an epic, worthy of the story it was telling. But somehow it never quite managed that level.

Reviewers noted that it did take some liberties with history in the cause of drama, but as the *National Review* pointed out, it "depends on too many clichés or near-clichés." The blacks were all composite characters, whereas Shaw had been a real person. And those composites, as many—like the *New Yorker*—noted, those composites were "based on white icons."

There was plenty to both praise and damn in the film. Praise, for a start, that it had been made at all, even though, the *New Yorker* said, it was "terribly literal-minded, with evenhanded pacing, and this fastidiousness mutes it emotionally. . . . *Glory* isn't a great film, but it's a good film on a great subject."

The *Christian Century* had trouble with its very 1960s (as opposed to 1860s) sensibility, "playing to an audience that has lived through a civil rights revolution." It was willing to concede, though, that "Shaw's story is important and enough of it comes through to fix his place in the twentieth century the way balladeers fixed it in the popular mind of the Civil War period."

It came close to running afoul of the *Cry Freedom* syndrome, telling a black story through white eyes. And it might well have done, except for the fact that the black actors were so much stronger than the white ones. As Shaw, Matthew Broderick "seems a bit slight for such a heroic role," The *Christian Century* decided. *Commonweal* was more caustic, saying "Casting Broderick marks no attempt to impose a white presence into a black story. And *People* felt he "never becomes the charismatic leader the movie needs him to be . . . lacks both physical and emotional stature." The *New Republic* deemed the casting of him "a gamble that fails." The *National Review* offered one of the few dissenting opinions. Agreeing that he wasn't "ideally cast," reviewer John Simon allowed that "he does try hard to be as far removed as possible from his usual smart-aleck, modern, New York self, and there is something appealing about the effort."

What really saved *Glory*, indeed, what made it rise above the pack, was the acting of Denzel, Morgan Freeman, Andre Braugher, and Jihmi Kennedy. As the black tentmates, they were powerful and understated. As The *National Review* summed them up, they "let us see consummate ensemble acting as one of the prime expressions of cooperation in a world lacerated by dissension," and *Vogue* succinctly decreed them to be "uniformly excellent." Freeman simply oozed charisma, while Denzel's spiky reading of Trip brought him completely to life.

During the scene around the campfire, on the night before the attack on Fort Wagner, Denzel improvised most of the speech where Trip talked about his life.

"There were very few scripted lines," he explained to *New York*. "I based my response on the personal history I had developed for the character—he was a runaway; he had lost his parents. I steeped myself in the reality I had formed for myself, so that when we got to that scene, it meant something more than just some words I was saying."

Earlier, when Trip was whipped, he said nothing, but the tears flowed quietly. That, too, was unrehearsed, Denzel admitted.

"It just happened. I was thinking that there is nothing else they can do to me. These were tears of defiance, really."

As he'd become Steve Biko, now he'd become Trip. As always, he'd researched the part, reading all he could find on the part that blacks played in the Civil War—slave narratives, historical archives, memoirs.

"I was happier making *Glory* than I've ever been working on a movie," Denzel told *California* in 1990. "We had a great deal of rehearsal time, which helped us lock in our characters, and I was playing a character that I really found interesting. He is somebody who makes people uncomfortable, because he's a racist. But he was made a racist by racism. He lived the way he had to live, doing whatever it took to survive. He wasn't afraid, which I admire."

His portrayal of Trip, especially during the whipping scene, was one that resonated with blacks, not only in America, but all through the world. As Nelson George wrote in *The Village Voice*, "As the whipping commences, Washington cuts Broderick one of those withering, contemptuous looks that brothers aim daily at racist or insensitive whites. . . . It's as if Denzel's visage communicated some transcendental aspect of our rage."

In that one moment, perhaps more than any other in the film, Denzel connected the dots through history, illuminating the fury of the black race at another race that would, in one way or another, be its master. However much the whipping might have troubled Shaw, he went ahead and ordered it, sticking to regulations. It wasn't his humiliation, his physical pain. Trip could deal with those things. His people had been doing that for many, many years. With one look he demanded not that the pain stop, but that he be afforded the respect of being a man.

And that, as George noted, "in the behavior box blacks are forced into means seeking white male approval." While Trip would ultimately do that—and while his descendants one hundred years later still wouldn't have that approval—he'd shown himself to be proud, upright, and honest with himself. It was a completely luminous segment, a shot that gave total insight not only into the character, but also a culture. After watching Trip's face, we knew exactly why these men were there, and why they were willing to risk their lives.

It was, in the literal sense, an inspired performance. Those improvised moments—the campfire speech, the look as Trip was being whipped—which seemed to come out of nowhere, were utterly incandescent, and helped make the film something much more than the sum of its parts. They not only illuminated Trip, but also the whole reason for the men being there, and the sad history that had brought them to that point. Everyone did a wonderful job, but to be able to say so much in a look or a few words indicated how much power Denzel had developed in his acting, and how much Trip, and *Glory* meant to him. The rage that smoldered constantly, the barely suppressed hatred, they all combined to push him into viewers' minds and keep him there. What resonated, long after the theaters were empty, wasn't Matthew Broderick, or even the marvelous Morgan Freeman, but Denzel. It was the charisma that he'd shown in *Cry Freedom*; he became the film. What he delivered was more than superb acting. He'd already proved he was quite capable of that. This time he raised his work to an entirely new level, the sort of performance that made you realize he was capable of doing anything onscreen.

His preparation and his acting ability truly paid off this time. The praise he received from the critics was universal. *Newsweek* called him "The charismatic Denzel Washington, oozing angry defiance," and termed his performance "extraordinary," while the *National Review*, pointing out that all the supporting players were superb, singled out Denzel for playing his part with "such clenched intensity, such primeval wariness about it that it becomes a kind of histrionic emancipation proclamation, soaring well above the scenarist's clichés." The *New Yorker* called him "the high-tension Bogart-Brando figure—sullen, cynical, smart," and there was a hair-trigger edge to his reading of the part, very 1960s, as the magazine continued: "He has a modern charge of ferocity; you're aware that it's anachronistic, yet it lifts you up." *Commonweal*, a little acerbically, said, "Washington juts his jaw in everyone's face; with his nonstop belligerence, bony face, and shaved head, he's Michael Jordan with menace, aching to fight anyone."

While the Academy probably didn't use phrases quite like that, they too were impressed by what they saw onscreen. Denzel was nominated for an Oscar for the second time, once more for best supporting actor.

And once again his competition was fierce—he was up against Dan Aykroyd, Martin Landau, Danny Aiello, and the mighty Marlon Brando (for *A Dry White Season*)—but this time he carried off the prize. What made the victory doubly sweet was the fact that not only was Denzel being lauded (only the fifth black actor ever to receive an Academy Award), but it was, at long last, an acceptance of those black Union soldiers.

Glory took three Oscars that night, but it wasn't the only award that Denzel would receive for his role in the film. He'd already managed to walk away with a Golden Globe for best supporting actor for playing Trip (Morgan Freeman won best actor for his work in *Driving Miss Daisy*), where he'd commented, "I really felt that I was going to win. A few years ago, I was here for *Cry Freedom* and I was calm. I didn't feel I would win. But this year, I really felt it."

But an award that he deemed "more important" than all the others was about to come his way— the NAACP Image Award for best supporting actor. It was an acknowledgment, not by the business, but by his own people, of the contribution he'd been able to make with his skill; no wonder that it meant so much.

By now there was a veritable flood of scripts for him to read, and people eager to cast him in films. He'd made three back-to-back, all quite intense, and he was ready for a change of pace. It came with the offer to be in *Heart Condition*, a comedy drama which at least let Denzel show that he didn't have to be utterly serious all the time.

However, before he was willing to sign on for the movie, he wanted certain changes made in the script. It wasn't a case of being a prima donna—he simply found some of the racial epithets excessive.

"Having done *Heart Condition* right after *Glory*, I couldn't deal with it," he explained. "I said there are too many racial slurs—cut it out, cut it out.

They had the word 'nigger' in there about fifty times."

It was a perfectly reasonable request, and it was done. In the final version the word occurred once, "and I still think it's too harsh." But when the film appeared the word was uttered more often than that—including one time from Denzel's own mouth—but yes, only once from a white man.

But he agreed to the part anyway, playing opposite British actor Bob Hoskins. The idea wasn't exactly original—a man receives a heart transplant, and the ghost of the donor returns to haunt him, but the racial angle of a black ghost dogging a bigoted white policeman added a neat touch.

Hoskins played Jack Mooney, an L.A. cop who was nothing less than a bigoted slob. He worked Vice, catching hookers, and held a huge grudge against attorney Napoleon Stone (Denzel). Crystal Garrity, Jack's former girlfriend, had left him for Stone, and in doing so, had gone back to prostitution.

Stone walked the edge of the law, but he wasn't intrinsically bad. But when Mooney saw Stone speeding one night, he broke off what he was doing to follow him. Just out of spite. At a private club Stone picked up Crystal and another girl, and Mooney took off in pursuit.

Stone managed to evade him on foot, taking time to drop the drugs the other girl had in her purse. Finally he was caught and arrested—but for what?

That was exactly what Mooney's commander wanted to know. No evidence, no suspicion. Stone was released, and Mooney suspended. But not before he and Crystal talked. She gave him some rolls of film she'd shot, to keep with all the others he collected, undeveloped, in a fishbowl.

That night Mooney had a heart attack, and would have died except for a miracle—a donor who was a perfect match came into the hospital, following an auto wreck.

It was the last heart he would have wanted. Stone's.

After months of recuperation, Mooney returned to work as a desk sergeant. He was off cigarettes, booze, and junk food on the orders of his doctor. But it couldn't last.

That was where Stone reentered the picture. Only Mooney could see him, a suave, urbane ghost who kept trying to keep Jack in order, while getting him to investigate—or avenge—Stone's murder.

It wasn't easy for Mooney, to say the least. He hated blacks in general, Stone in particular. And being seen talking to the air made people wonder if he was losing his mind.

But eventually he went along with it. The first step was to find Crystal, who'd seemingly disappeared. But she was still working for the same pimp as a call girl.

Mooney and Stone located him. Now Mooney needed to change his image, appear rich. Stone led him to his secret stash of money, and made him spend some of it—on a makeover, new clothes, a decent haircut, a good car. Now he was ready.

Posing as a wealthy businessman, he contacted the pimp, Graham, and arranged a date with Crytal at an expensive hotel. It went better than Mooney could have expected—Crystal was still in love with him. But when, at Stone's urging, he asked her about the murder, she wouldn't tell him anything, and ran from the room.

Following her, he found himself arrested, briefly, and questioned by his superiors. If he wasn't very careful, he was going to be leaving the force for psychiatric reasons.

He was stymied—or was he? Sitting at home, wondering where he could go, Mooney had an inspiration. He developed all the film in the fishbowl. Somewhere in there were the rolls Crystal had given him on the night she was arrested with Stone.

The pictures told the story, not of Stone's murder, but what led up to it. Two prostitutes—one of them Crystal—cavorting with a man, a senator famous for his antidrug legislation, who'd supposedly died of natural causes—except there he was, on the bed, with a crack pipe in his hand. Now he understood what was going on. Mooney asked his colleagues to pull the senator's autopsy file, and see if the body had been been tested for drugs.

What he needed now was to find Crystal, who'd

seemingly vanished again. But he did have one lead. She had a record of Malibu parking tickets, and he'd seen beach tar on her feet.

So he set out to walk the beach at Malibu and look for her.

By now Jack and Stone had become closer. There was a fragile bond, a trust, between them. Or, at the very least, a tolerance.

But it was thin. And when Mooney found Crystal, and learned that she was scared to tell the truth because of her baby—Stone's baby—that was the end.

He drove off, crazily, and above the ocean, he and Stone told each other some painful truths. Mooney collapsed. He was rejecting his heart.

He woke in the hospital, Stone's ghost next to him. And called to check his answering machine. There was one message, from Crystal. Mooney had to be at an abandoned house, with the pictures, by eight, or Graham would kill her. And the baby.

It was already after seven.

Sneaking out of the hospital, still weak, he stole a police car, and reached the house just after eight. Graham had had his henchmen inject Crystal with a small dose of heroin, enough to keep her pliable.

Now it was down to Mooney. Stone led the way, checking corners and rooms, the ghost giving Jack the edge, until he was able to rescue Crystal and her son. Even then, escaping wasn't easy. And Jack would have been dead if Graham's cellular phone hadn't rung and given him away. With a final blast of the shotgun, Stone had freed Crystal and avenged himself.

Mooney and Crystal married. Stone, unseen by any except the groom, was there to wish them well. Stone and Jack were friends. And all lived (or died) happily ever after.

It wasn't a highlight in either Denzel's or Hoskins's body of work. The movie had the potential to be good, and with two such actors it could have been *very* good, but in the end it couldn't overcome the weight of the clichés, both of the script and direction.

Heart Condition didn't make much of a splash, either with critics or audiences. It appeared, then vanished, fairly quickly, which in many ways was a blessing. Although not a complete embarrassment—with Denzel and Hoskins it could never be quite that—it certainly wasn't something to be remembered with glowing pride.

The best it could manage was a few, brief reviews, which varied from downright hatred to mild amusement. The *Nation* called it "A comedy without laughs, a thriller without suspense, a morality tale without ethics," adding that it didn't "even give you the pleasure of watching something actively bad—all its faults are sins of omission." *Newsweek* deemed it to be "a gimmick masquerading as a story," which was plotted "so lazily you almost forget there's a mystery to be cracked."

On the other hand, *People* felt it became "oddly involving," and while admitting that it "never quite overcomes its status as a novelty number, yet it maintains a comic integrity," to end up "with an unexpected heart, functioning precariously but doing its job."

As it was, *People* turned out to be the only magazine to mention Denzel's contribution to the movie, citing the way that, as a ghost, he "wordlessly displays his pain at being able to observe life but not take part in it."

So what, finally, was the point of it? That it wanted to do the right thing was evident, but along the way, it just didn't end up having what was necessary to succeed. Really, it was little better than a glorified television movie, with slightly more graphic language. Perhaps the best that can be said about it is that it gave Denzel a chance to flex his comic muscles; the only shame was that he couldn't get to display them in a better setting. As an experiment, it was a failure, and sadly, not even a glorious one.

For the most part it vanished without a trace— just for the best. But the press did attempt to make a story out of it, and the way Mooney openly felt about blacks—at least in the beginning of the movie. They tried to create a tempest; however, it never quite made it out of the teacup. Asked for his opinion on black reaction to the film, Denzel calmly replied, "I don't know—the black community doesn't meet at my house on Wednesday nights.''

Mercifully for everyone concerned, the attempt at scandal-mongering died as swiftly as the film itself. But that couldn't be said of what came next. *Mo' Better Blues* was exactly what Denzel needed now.

SIX

Spike Lee had acquired a reputation in the film industry as the leading black director. Indeed, as far as any kind of commercial success went, he was the *only* black director. *She's Gotta Have It*, *School Daze*, and *Do the Right Thing* had all served to establish his reputation. Not only did he entertain, but he said something about the feelings and conditions of blacks in America. The fact that he was often outspoken, deliberately controversial, and sometimes eager to bite the corporate hand that fed him, only served to heighten his image. He was a person who could make things happen, a director who could be bankrolled even without huge stars, someone whose work would be seen, and which would at the very least be interesting.

He'd seen *'Round Midnight* and *Bird*, films about jazz musicians that had been directed by whites, and he felt that something was wrong with them. At its heart, jazz was *black* American music. His own father was a jazz musician. Spike Lee felt that *he* should make a jazz film. Something that highlighted not the romance of the music world, but its bitter realities. *Mo' Better Blues* (originally to have been titled *A Love Supreme*, after the classic John Coltrane track, until Coltrane's widow removed permission), was intended to be that film, with Lee's father, Bill, writing the score, and real jazz players—trumpeter Terence Blanchard and Branford Marsalis's group—providing the music.

For his model, he took the great trumpeter Miles Davis (who has since died), and wove the story of Bleek Gilliam, someone driven to succeed in a way that most people couldn't understand. For the role there was one person he wanted, someone who was already acknowledged as the leading black actor of his generation—Denzel.

". . . I knew Denzel was the person for the part. I wrote the movie for him because I wanted to use the rapport he has with the female audience. Women love him."

He recognized Denzel's charisma, and wanted to put it to work, as he told *American Film.* "It's Denzel's movie. He's magnetic, he's a great actor. . . . I remember going to see him in *Checkmates* on Broadway, and the minute he came onstage, all the women started oohing and aahing and that kinda stuff. Women love them some Denzel." And, he added later, talking to *New York*, "I think this role will free Denzel from playing these great, heroic, stoic types."

And Denzel was very happy to agree to the part, one that was, indeed, quite different for him. In fact, he said, "It was just about the easiest job I've had in terms of filming. I just had to play it right and look like a musician." Lee had written a good script, the movie made its points well, and there was plenty for him to get his teeth into as an actor.

"I play this very selfish, self-centered, egotistical trumpet player," he explained in *Ebony*, "who puts his music before anything else in his life."

It had all the possibilities of being exactly what he needed at this point—a star vehicle. In *Glory* and *Cry Freedom* he indicated the things he was capable of, but hadn't really had a chance to develop to their fullest. The fact was that Denzel was more than ready, and more than due, for a starring role. He'd been in the shadows as a supporting actor and a co-star long enough—maybe too long. Now he was ready to step into the limelight alone.

To prepare himself for the role of Bleek, Denzel did two things. He spent time with Davis, absorbing some of the man's intensity and concentration, and saying later, "Miles is crazy! His sound was so sweet, his soul just came through that horn. He found his sound . . . The Prince of Darkness."

And he learned to play the trumpet. Denzel never learned to play well—that was an impossibility, given the short time he had—but enough to look convincing onscreen.

"All the playing you see is me. Not all the playing you *hear*, but all the playing you see."

That, however, was perfectly typical of him. A poor imitation was no substitute; he had to become the person he was portraying. The work paid off; Denzel definitely became Bleek Gilliam.

As a boy, Bleek hadn't exactly been a dedicated musician. He'd rather have been out playing ball with the friends who came to his Brooklyn front stoop and shouted for him to join them. His easy-going father would have let him go. His mother, however, was adamant. She knew the boy needed discipline in his life, and she was going to provide it, making him finish his daily practice before he could go out and play.

By the time he was an adult, it had all been worthwhile. Bleek had blossomed into a trumpeter of gigantic talent, leading his own band, playing at a good club, making good money.

Lines formed outside the place, Beneath the Underdog, every night to hear him. He gave the people what he wanted them to hear, his own take on jazz.

Music was his focus, his life. Anything, and everything, else came a distant second.

That included his love life. He had two women,

Indigo and Clarke, both of whom loved him in their own different ways, but while the sex was good, even great, neither of them had a chance of capturing his mind or heart.

Bleek was managed by one of his childhood friends, Giant (played by Spike Lee, who loves to appear in his own films). But he wasn't a particularly effective manager. He had a gambling problem (that wouldn't have been a massive problem, except that he lost consistently), and he'd tied the band into their contract at the club. Now they were playing to packed houses, asking for more money, and there was no way the owners were willing to pay.

This meant that tensions were running high in the group. Bleek managed to keep order through his iron will, but that could only last for so long. The music they played was something very special, but they all had to live.

Bleek, too, wanted more money. Not so much because he needed it—he had a wonderful Brooklyn apartment, dressed well, and seemed to live exactly the way he wanted—but as a measure of his increasing status.

Still, the owners weren't about to budge for any reason.

For Shadow (Wesley Snipes), the sax player, it was all reaching a head. He knew he had the ability to lead a band, and he possessed his own vision of what would make it successful. At least, that was what he kept telling everyone.

What he kept saying to Bleek—as did the other members of the band—was that they needed a new manager. And in his heart, Bleek knew it was true, however much he wanted to be loyal to his old friend.

The truth was, Giant wasn't very effective. He couldn't get them more money from the club, or out of their contract. They were stuck.

Tensions were high all around. They grew even higher when both of Bleek's girlfriends showed up at the club, on the same night, wearing identical dresses he'd bought them in Paris. He visited one, then the other, trying to be diplomatic, and unseen.

Shadow noticed an opportunity. He knew Clarke was a singer, one who wanted to sing professionally. While Bleek was with Indigo, he sat with her, promised her a place in the band he was going to put together. Very soon. And that night he went home with her.

Giant was losing a lot of money. On a bike ride, he asked Bleek for a loan to pay his gambling debts—another loan. Bleek agreed, although it would take him some time to raise the kind of money needed. And at the same time, he fired him as manager.

But time had run out for Giant. On his way home, a car door opened in his path, forcing him off the bicycle. He was dragged into a car by two thugs, who broke two of his fingers—as a lesson. Their boss needed his money—now.

With his friend gone, Bleek's world was slowly falling apart. He'd lost one girlfriend to his saxophone player, and now the other one, Indigo, the sensible teacher, was rejecting him. His mind confused them. Which one was he in bed with? Their faces changed before his eyes. Which one was there? Or was either one there at all?

He was still playing well, at the top of his form on the horn, still pleasing the crowds who came to see him night after night. On the surface it looked good, but the foundations were crumbling. He couldn't get the club managers to budge on the contract, either, and the rumbles of discontent from the band were growing louder.

It all reached a climax in the alley behind the club. Giant had come to see Bleek, to talk, and discover when Bleek might have his money.

Before Bleek appeared, though, the thugs arrived, and began to beat Giant in a thorough, professional manner. When Bleek showed up, still carrying his horn, and tried to stop them, they began to work him over, too. Not just his body. They slashed the horn across his lips, cutting them terribly, then pounded him into unconsciousness and left the two friends side by side on the garbage sacks before anyone could call the police.

For months after his recovery, Bleek didn't leave his apartment. The beating had left him a broken man, both pysically and mentally. Finally, though, he did come out one rainy night, and headed into Manhattan, taking his trumpet with him. To Dizzy's, the jazz club where his old band, now under the leadership of Shadow, and with Clarke as singer, was playing. He was going to sit in with them. The first person he saw was Giant, now working as the doorman there.

Inside, the crowds were being entertained by something that was light and frothy, music that wasn't really jazz. Slowly he walked to the stage, to a round of applause, raised his horn—and after just a few notes, it became obvious that he'd lost it. Completely. Bleek couldn't play anymore.

Defeated, deserted by the only thing he'd had any certainty about in life, he was lost. Which left him only one thing.

He went to Indigo's apartment. They hadn't talked in months. She'd called to see how he was recovering, and he'd never replied. She'd loved him, and he'd only used her. Why should she want him now?

But she still loved him, and, for the first time, he really needed her.

They moved in together, had a baby, married. Bleek was no longer a musician. His focus had shifted, widened to include more of the world.

Their son grew, and began to learn the trumpet. They moved into an apartment identical to the one where Bleek had lived as a boy.

The youngster's friends came around, tempting him out to play ball when he should have been practicing. No, his mother insisted, he needed to finish his lesson first. But Bleek stepped in, and let the boy go.

History was not about to repeat itself.

It wasn't Spike Lee's best work, by any stretch of the imagination. In fact, the word most used by reviewers to describe it was "disappointing." Or, as John Simon wrote in *National Review*, with *Mo' Better Blues* "Unfortunately, what we get is mo' worse." He found little to redeem the film, whether it was the dialogue "that creaks along most of the time," or the long closing montage, "which is reminiscent in style of the commercials Lee has been making for TV." Nor was Simon fond of the "arbitrary bits of heavy-handed symmetry Spike keeps imposing over and over again, more like elementary geometry than enlightened filmmaking." Not even the sex scenes convinced him, being "neither artistic nor erotic."

There was no doubt that *Mo' Better Blues* was an ambitious project, both as a jazz movie and a love story. And that, perhaps, was its ultimate downfall. Lee just attempted to put too much in, rather than tightening his focus. Even *Ebony*, normally a staunch supporter of his work, had plenty of criticisms, admitted that "Lee wants to cram in so much . . . that he ends up glossing over the essentials. . . . For the only time in his remarkable career, Spike Lee has failed to tell it like it is."

Ultimately, the story's sprawl ruined its impact. And in its ending, just too neatly tied to its beginning, Lee rounded things off *too* well. In real life, the ends don't always tie up neatly, the circle isn't always made. Was it even necessary to show that happening in Bleek's life? Yes, need and love changed him, opened him up, but was it worthwhile to encapsulate a dozen years into a few minutes to show that? Somehow it made the power of what had gone before more diffuse.

The *New Republic* dismissed it as "disjointed, overwrought . . . stale . . . full of patches, snags, and awkward jumps." To *America* it seemed that Lee "has faltered badly in this latest effort." Although the reviewer did concede that "The characters are interesting, the exposition economical," he found the conclusion "too neat and too phony." He also felt that the scene where Giant and Bleek are beaten "yields to the Hollywood pornography of violence," a view that was echoed by *New York*, where the critic decided it "goes on way past the moment of making its point about gratuitous brutality."

Still, all in all, the failure remained noble. Lee's reach had simply exceeded his grasp. And, to be fair, the critics' comments did seem to contain a certain element of backlash toward Lee, one that also ended up catching Denzel in its wake. The part of Bleek had been a magnificent showcase for his talents, but in the end what he received were mixed reviews.

Cosmopolitan summed it up best: "Denzel Washington is a superstar waiting to happen. Blessed with sexy good looks and a formidable range of emotion, he has been acclaimed . . ." which was all perfectly true, but even such a gushing opening had to admit "It is by no means certain . . . that this . . . will be the vehicle that takes him to the top." And *People* said, "It's a shame that Washington's ability to create a unique, engrossing character was so badly compromised in this film." *National Review*'s opinion was that "Denzel Washington, an excellent actor, doesn't find his bearings as Bleek," while the *New Republic* felt he played the part "as well as is possible." While *Newsweek* summed the film up as "an urgent, confused movie about work and love," it felt that "Bleek cuts a cool, romantic profile onstage (how could he not, he's played by Denzel Washington)."

And while the role was meant to be a romantic lead, it wasn't necessarily romantic in the traditional sense; Bleek was in love with music, forsaking all else for it. Only when it abandoned him did he learn to love other things, and, more specifically, people. Over the course of the film he became human, instead of the insulated, isolated machine he had been.

Of course, there was sex in the film. With the mix of characters, that was inevitable, and it did lead to an early clash between Denzel and Lee.

"I didn't like the love scenes, at all," Denzel admitted. "That was the most tension-filled time on the set, 'cause I didn't like it—it's too fleshy for my taste. I don't like feeling the way I felt during those scenes. And he (Lee) knew, 'cause we always had arguments on those days. Those were things I didn't want to shoot."

Once those disputes were patched up, things went smoothly, and Denzel was pleased at "getting to work with my contemporaries. Spike and I worked very closely, and I did more improvisation in this movie than I ever have."

It should have been a high-water mark in Denzel's career, and, had it been a better film, might have helped catapult him to huge stardom much earlier. But certainly, there was no fault to be found in his portrayal of Bleek. He'd taken a character who, at first, seemed somewhat two-dimensional, missing that vital human element, and turned him into a living, breathing human being, someone the audience could really care about. That in itself was quite a feat, since the emotional distance at which Bleek kept himself from others made him hard to pin down. In lesser hands he'd have come across as a very wooden figure. As it was, it needed the special charisma that Denzel could unleash on-screen. He made Bleek fill a stage, made him rounded and completely alive there. The audience in the cinema could easily understand how all eyes would be riveted on him, whether he was playing along with the band, or taking flight on a solo, or even singing and rapping on the song "Mo' Better Blues." And after Bleek's beating, when the ability and the confidence was gone, he was able to portray how lost the character was without resorting to many words. He pared it down to an expression, to the body language he used. As he'd done with every role he'd undertaken, Denzel got inside Bleek, under his skin. He knew him as well as— and for the duration of the shooting, maybe even better than—he knew himself. It wasn't Denzel Washington up there playing Bleek. It was simply Bleek acting out his life. He'd done better than anyone else could have, and Denzel was quite rightly happy with his work. But for now, there were fresh challenges to face.

SEVEN

It was time for a break, however short, from making movies. The stage was where Denzel had begun, and it was a type of acting he still loved—very immediate, full of life, full of chances and accidents. When he'd appeared in *Checkmates*, *The Village Voice*'s critic had thought it would be interesting to see him in Shakespeare. Now he'd have his chance.

Denzel had been approached by Joseph Papp to take the title role in *Richard III*, to be staged in Central Park as part of the New York Shakespeare Festival. Papp had seen him in *Checkmates*, and come away impressed.

"He was suave, graceful, and attractive," Papp told *New York*. "He has the supreme confidence to twist men and women around his finger. He can come across as both regal and ordinary."

The opportunity was one that many actors wait a lifetime to be offered. Denzel was only thirty-five.

But whether it was exhaustion, or feeling himself on unfamiliar ground after being used to movie sets, the performance that he turned in left the reviewers unmoved; one called him "surprisingly . . . muted."

Certainly, *New York* wasn't kind to him. Critic John Simon admitted that he was "an actor of noteworthy achievement, and, I believe, even more promise," and that "Given the right role . . . he is electrifying and unforgettable." But, he was forced to wonder "what in his background . . . could have prepared him for a Shakespearian lead? . . . This Richard speaks in something perilously close to a monotone, with the voice tending to become shrill, suggesting unease. . . . Worst of all, Washington misses Richard's humor." And to *Backstage*, "The actor's lack of command of the verse doesn't help. The soliloquies lose power when Washington runs out of breath by the end of the line or phrase."

The problem certainly wasn't a lack of desire on Denzel's part, or even a lack of talent. This production simply didn't work well; it never quite came together. And, interestingly enough, it was the last time he'd appear in theater for a few years.

If *Richard III* was an attempt to broaden his acting palette in a more classical direction, his next film took him to another extreme—Denzel Washington as action hero. *Ricochet* was about as big a

Denzel Washington pictured with some of his co-stars from the Emmy-winning NBC television series, *St. Elsewhere*. (*Photofest*)

Kevin Kline teams up with Denzel in *Cry Freedom*. (*Photofest*)

Washington played a soldier in the Civil War in the critically acclaimed film, *Glory*. (*The Gamma Liaison Network*)

Denzel and his *Glory* co-stars, Matthew Broderick and Morgan Freeman, at the film's premiere. (*Outline Press Syndicate Inc.*)

Geena Davis presented Denzel with a Best
Supporting Actor Oscar for his role in *Glory*.
(*AP/Wide World Photos*)

Denzel pictured with Spike Lee, his director in *Mo'
Better Blues* and *Malcolm X*.
(*The Gamma Liaison Network*)

Washington received rave reviews for his role as the charismatic leader in *Malcolm X*. (*Sygma Photo News*)

Julia Roberts shared the screen with Denzel for the film adaptation of John Grisham's *The Pelican Brief*. (*Photofest*)

Washington portrayed a homophobic lawyer in the groundbreaking film *Philadelphia*. (*Photofest*)

Denzel and Tom Hanks at the premiere of *Philadelphia*. Hanks won an Academy Award for his role in the AIDS drama. (*Outline Press Syndicate Inc.*)

Denzel stars in William Shakespeare's *Much Ado About Nothing*. (*Sygma Photo News*)

Denzel, pictured with his mother, received a degree from Fordham University in 1991. (*Outline Press Syndicate Inc.*)

Denzel clowns around with his son, John David, at a charity event for the Children's Defense Fund. (*Celebrity Photo Agency*)

Washington grills Lou Diamond Phillips in the 1996 film *Courage Under Fire*. (*Photofest*)

Denzel and wife Pauletta at the world premiere of
Courage Under Fire in Beverly Hills.
(*AP/Wide World Photos*)

Denzel and
Whitney Houston,
his co-star in Penny
Marshall's remake
of the 1947 film *The
Bishop's Wife* (now
titled *The Preacher's
Wife*) at an awards
ceremony. (*AP/Wide
World Photos*)

change from Steve Biko or Bleek Gilliam as he could find.

Nick Styles (Denzel) was a rookie cop in Los Angeles, one with some ambition. The son of a Watts minister, he was attending law school, not wanting to spend the rest of his life on the streets. He'd gone the way of law enforcement; his childhood friend Odessa (Ice-T) had turned to crime—dealing drugs, stealing cars, and then manufacturing crack. But, as they'd find, the bond between them remained tighter than they ever could have realized.

Patrolling a community fair one night, Nick and his partner heard shots, and investigated. They came across a major drug deal being held up by gunmen, and as Blake (John Lithgow), one of the robbers, tried to escape, Nick cornered him. Blake took a hostage, and wanted Nick to put down his weapon. He did, then stripped to his shorts to show he wasn't wearing body armor or carrying a second gun. Then, just as Blake thought he was getting clear, Nick pulled a derringer from his shorts and shot him in the knee.

It was a remarkable arrest, made even more remarkable by the fact that a bystander caught it on videotape, which immediately aired on local television. Nick Styles was suddenly the most popular man in L.A. He was promoted to detective, and, once he'd finished his law degree, made into an assistant district attorney.

Blake, in jail, could only seethe and swear revenge.

Nick's career continued to rise in a bright arc. He prosecuted, and won, the Night Strangler case, which brought him back into the public eye, and began to move into politics, announcing as his personal cause the making of the Watts Towers into a community center for local youth. With the patronage of a local black councilman, it was going to happen.

Blake, meanwhile, was establishing himself as someone not to be crossed in a maximum security facility. In a fight organized by the prisoners, he killed his cellmate, and ingratiated himself with the Aryan Brotherhood. He had his plan for revenge on Styles, and the steps were already in motion. His sidekick, Kim, switched Blake's dental records for those of another prisoner, Jesse. Now all Blake had to do was escape.

His opportunity came at a parole hearing, where his cohorts in the Brotherhood just happened to be working—with power tools. From somewhere, Blake had obtained a gun. He shot the chairman of the parole board, stole his clothes. His friends overpowered the guards. Disguised, with hostages, Blake and Jesse walked out, leaving a trail of bodies behind them.

Away from the prison, they met up with Kim, who had a car waiting. Blake killed Jesse, sending his body over a cliff in the getaway vehicle, which burned. All that was left of Jesse was his teeth. From the dental records, so far as anyone knew, Blake had escaped, then died.

Nick had organized a telethon at his father's church to raise money for the youth center. He'd also visited Odessa at his crack plant, warning him to keep his dealers away from the center when it opened, that it was sacred ground.

While the successful telethon was going on, Blake entered Nick's house, posing as an electric company repairman who was there to fix a supposed power outage. It was a show of his power, his ability to do what he wanted.

The final, anonymous donation of ten thousand dollars in cash put the telethon over the top. The center would happen. As the evening ended, the councilman said he'd go to the night deposit with the money.

The next morning Nick received a phone call. The money was gone. So was the councilman, who had supposedly committed suicide dressed in drag, leaving a note implying that he and Nick had molested children on a recent trip to Florida.

Nick's nightmare was just beginning. The D.A. wanted to know what was happening, and Nick honestly had no idea.

On his way home, he was kidnapped by Blake and Kim, drugged, and filmed having sex with a hooker. Two days later he was left on the street. Now he knew Blake wasn't dead, but no one wanted to believe him. The records proved that the man no longer existed.

Alison, Nick's wife, wanted to believe, but it was hard. What he was saying stretched credibility. Even more so when hospital bloodwork showed that he had gonorrhea.

Nick spent a long, drunken night on the couch. When he woke, there was a tape in the VCR with a note that read "Play Me." It showed Blake—in Nick's house—standing over his daughters with an ax. Nick ran upstairs. The kids and his wife had gone to a show in the park.

Still in his bathrobe, carrying a gun, Nick ran there, almost killing a clown he believed was Blake. And all of it, of course, was captured on videotape.

The district attorney had no choice but to suspend him, particularly when the video of Nick having sex with the hooker was shown on the television news.

But his old partner came to the rescue. Doing some digging, he'd learned that Blake and his buddy were supposed to pick up false passports at an Aryan bookstore. They decided to pay the shop a visit.

Kim arrived while they were there, and Nick's partner took off after him. In an alley, Blake killed him, then tossed the empty gun to Nick, who, unthinking, caught it. Now his prints were on a murder weapon. It was looking increasingly as if a dead man was getting his revenge.

In utter desperation, Nick had only one option And there was only one man who could help him now. It was Odessa, who thought he was crazy, but agreed.

Nick climbed to the top of the building where Odessa manufactured his crack. As the TV mini-cams shot live footage, he ranted and raved, and threatened to kill himself.

That was more than Blake, watching in a bar, could stand. He wanted Styles to suffer for a long time, not die yet. He and Kim went to the scene.

Odessa's henchmen grabbed Kim, but left Blake alone as he wandered through the crowd. As a finale, Nick set fire to the building, escaping through an air chute. As the flames rose, Blake was summoned to a pay phone, where Odessa instructed him to go to the Watts Towers.

Kim was already there, tied to the structure. Blake shot him. Nick was there too, waiting, and up on the girders the two of them began a life-and-death struggle. Inevitably, it was on live television, offering incontrovertible proof that Nick Styles hadn't lost his mind; Blake was still very much alive.

Not for too long, though. A final fall from the towers left him impaled on a spike. The nightmare was over, and Nick walked away from the cameras. Forever.

All in all, it was a strange movie. From a straight, suspenseful thriller that also offered strongly satirical comments on the way the media could make and break personalities and careers, it took a sharp turn into the unreal and unlikely.

Why, one had to wonder, would Odessa allow his drug factory to be destroyed just to satisfy Nick? What did he get out of all of this? How did Nick know his apparent suicide attempt would draw Blake to the scene? And what had been the point of dressing Blake and his opponent as gladiators for their prison fight?

It was a shame. A lot of the film was well done, drawing in the audience only to leave one shaking one's head at the end. It had become ridiculous, virtually comedy.

It really couldn't be saved, although the lead actors tried hard. John Lithgow, best known for playing good guys, was a very powerful, credible psychopath who simply oozed evil. Ice-T, as Odessa, offered some light relief, but always teetering on the edge of violence. And, until he turned into something vaguely resembling a superhero, Denzel was utterly real as Nick Styles.

However, the world just didn't seem to be ready for the idea of Denzel as an action hero; at least, not in a movie like this, which strained credibility way beyond the breaking point. Denzel could have been absolute perfection in the role (and he was, as always, very good), and it wouldn't have salvaged this film. Audiences didn't buy it, reviewers didn't bother with it, and in the end, that was all for the best. People didn't care about Denzel as Schwar-zenegger or Stallone. The wanted to see the man *act* and look good.

He himself wasn't happy with it, but for different reasons. He knew it wasn't a good film. It was there, it offered another starring role, which meant more visibility. But when he had a chance to see the finished product, he came to a decision. He re-alized, ". . . I can't—this is not me. I can't do this kind of movie. 'Cause this is mindless violence. I can't be a part of this. . . ."

It wasn't a case of stardom at any price. He knew that now. Better to do it his own way, to be real and true to his principles, to be himself, rather than try and manufacture some image that could never work anyway, since his heart wouldn't be in it. It wasn't what people wanted from him, and it cer-tainly wasn't what he wanted from himself.

That point was driven home further by his next role, in *Mississippi Masala*. Denzel had been ap-proached with the script, and as soon as he read it, he knew he wanted to be involved. The problem was that, far from being a large, or even small, Hol-lywood production, this was being shot on a very tight budget. The producers couldn't afford to pay him anywhere near the amount he'd normally re-ceive.

But for a wonderful role in what looked like it might be an outstanding movie, he was more than willing to work around that. In the end, Denzel agreed to appear for one quarter of his regular salary.

The mere fact that he was on board meant that *Mississippi Masala* had a much better chance of being noticed by the critics, who loved Denzel in a real role, and who, it turned out, would mostly share his enthusiasm for the film.

It was a love story of two cultures, black American and (East) Indian, which also explored the prejudices of different races, their insularity and traditional views.

Jay (Roshan Seth) had been a successful lawyer in Uganda. He was Indian in his coloring and values, but he'd been born and raised in Uganda; it was his only home, a place he loved. So when the dictator Idi Amin expelled the Indians in 1972, and Jay was forced to leave with his wife and daughter, Mina, he became a lost man.

The family moved around, to England and America, unable to settle, because there was no new place that could ever become home to Jay. He wrote to the new Ugandan government, trying to gain compensation for all he'd lost, but over the years he'd heard nothing.

By 1990 they were living in Greenwood, Mississippi. Their residence was two motel rooms, part of the Monte Cristo, owned and run by other Indians, their extended family in America. Jay did almost nothing. His wife has blossomed into a businesswoman, running a liquor store, and Mina

(Sarita Choudhury), now twenty-four, contented herself by working at the motel, cleaning rooms and helping behind the desk.

She'd been to the grocery store, picking up milk for a wedding, and was on her way home when she met Demetrius Williams (Denzel) by accidentally rear-ending his van. The car Mina was driving was wrecked, but the van—and all the people—escaped without injury.

Demetrius, with his friend Tyrone, ran a carpet-cleaning business. It wasn't making him rich, but it was honest work that paid the bills, and enough to let him look after his aging father, who refused to give up his job as a waiter in a white-owned restaurant.

At an Indian wedding, Mina was asked out by Harry, the most eligible Indian boy in town. She accepted, and they slipped away to a black club. There Mina saw Demetrius again.

But Demetrius saw someone, too. Alicia, a former girlfriend who'd left town to make it as a singer, and who was back visiting, putting on all manners of airs and graces.

To make her jealous, he asked Mina to dance, and they held each other close during a slow song. That infuriated Harry, who left, which meant that Demetrius ended up taking Mina home.

At the time, they didn't seem to take each other seriously. But Demetrius stuck in Mina's mind, and she called him during the week. He asked her over the following Sunday to meet his family, and celebrate his father's birthday.

The day seemed a huge success. His family appeared to like her, and his Aunt Rose told her a little about the young man, how he could have gone to college, but instead, following his mother's death, he chose to stay home with his father and younger brother, take out a loan, and start his own business. He was, she said, a good man.

Later in the afternoon, Demetrius and Mina went for a walk along the bayou, began kissing, and a romance was born.

Instinctively, they both kept it quiet, knowing there'd be disapproval. They were both people of color, but that didn't make it all right. They were each expected to marry "their own kind" and Greenwood was like any other small town where rumors flew like the wind.

Demetrius asked her to go with him to Biloxi, a town that was a night away, so they could be together. She agreed, lying to her parents about where she'd be.

Not that Jay was really noticing. After eighteen years he'd received word from the Ugandan government that his case would be heard. But the court date was only a week away, and he physically had to be present there.

In Biloxi the young couple was carefree, happy, and openly together. But there was trouble on the horizon. Some of Mina's male relatives were down there, and thought they saw her with Demetrius. The next morning, when they noticed his van at a motel, they knew they hadn't been mistaken.

One of them, Anil, hammered on the door of the room. Demetrius let him in, and Anil saw Mina scurrying from the bed. A fight ensued, and both Demetrius and Mina were arrested. It was a scandal. Mina's parents forbade her to see Demetrius. But if she suffered, what happened to him was even worse.

Within a matter of days, he'd lost most of his local clients. As if that wasn't enough, the bank announced they would foreclose on his loan in two weeks. He'd stepped outside the prescribed path for a black man, and now he was going to pay the price.

He tried to see her, but couldn't.

Then Jay made a decision. He would take his family back to Uganda, the place that meant so much to him.

As they packed, Mina walked out. She took Anil's Lincoln, and went looking for Demetrius, finding him trying to drum up business in a neighboring town.

He was in no mood to talk to her. Involvement with Mina had ruined his life. But finally she made him stop, and listen to her. They talked for a long time, and made their decision. They were going somewhere, anywhere, together, to start life anew.

Demetrius called his father to tell him, and Mina

spoke to her mother. Neither was even going back for their clothes or possessions; if they did that, they'd never leave.

Jay returned to Uganda, briefly. He learned that his oldest friend, an African, had died soon after the Asian expulsion. And while he still loved the place, it had stopped being home. Where he needed to be was with his wife. He didn't even stay long enough for the court case.

It was absolutely nothing like the movies coming out of Hollywood. There was no gloss, no quick and easy morality to *Mississippi Masala*. Even its slow, lazy pacing kept it apart from most American product.

The film lived up to everything Denzel had hoped it would be when he agreed to participate in it. In a country that was supposed to be an ethnic melting pot, the races were deliberately isolating themselves. Culture and tradition could count for much more than love.

Neither Demetrius nor Mina was especially heroic, or even single-minded. They had their lives, he with his own business, she drifting, when they met each other. The spark just happened. They were ordinary people, living in an ordinary manner. Making something greater out of them was part of director Mira Nair's success with the movie. It showed that love could conquer all—even the past.

As Jack Matthews described it in *New York News-*

day, *Mississippi Masala* was one of those rare events "that transport us to places we've never been, introduce us to cultures we've never known, to lives we've never imagined, and return us to our seats uplifted and enlightened." To *Glamour*, it was simply "exotic, funny, and definitely worth seeing," and the *New Yorker* dubbed it "easygoing exotica." *Newsweek* found it to be a "lively, serious comedy" with an "affectionate satirical spirit," Denzel and Sarita Choudhury making a "smashingly sensual Romeo and Juliet." While the reviewer admitted that the film had "a few bumpy, melodramatic patches," it was, in the end, a "smart, appealing movie." And *Vogue* summed it up as "good-hearted and optimistic," with "an off-killer charm, because it is as much about displacement and homesickness as it is about love."

That last point was raised by a number of critics. *Film Quarterly* felt that the romance "is in fact upstaged by the more complex and interesting story of the father." In fact, the *National Catholic Reporter* found that that aspect of *Mississippi Masala* had "far more emotional resonance than the love story," deciding that it "makes us reflect on the historical damage done to two communities, one dreaming of an India they have never seen, the other of an Africa they know little about."*America* took a slightly different tack, as Richard A. Blake concluded that the point of the film was "surviving the onslaught of memories attacking from within."

There were some who, although finding it "surprisingly humorous," like *Film Quarterly*, also had problems with the film's "simplistic solutions to the problems that the two protagonists face." *New York* also had reservations, not so much about that, but about the film as a whole. Defining it as "a nice movie," David Denby was forced to write, in the end, "I wish the picture were better made, with some ease and flow and some show-business smarts."

But that was the exception, rather than the rule. Most, like *Maclean's*, were happy with what was onscreen, calling it "utterly fresh and charming . . . also profoundly interesting," a "gently exhilirating tale of interracial romance."

And, naturally, Denzel was widely praised for his understated performance in the film. *People*, in a rave review, felt it would "make a believer out of anyone who ever doubted that he is an A-list movie star and sex symbol. This man is debonair. And magnetic. And he has an innate sweetness like Henry Fonda's but with even more steel." To *Maclean's* he was "charismatic," and "reveals a quality of tenderness that he has never shown before: the camera adores him." The *National Catholic Reporter* predicted that his "star quality should assure an audience," as he "communicates tenderness and strength." And to *America*, "Denzel Washington has become a major star, and his balance of easygoing charm and intensity make Demetrius believable and likable." The *New Yorker* happily added to all the plaudits with, "Throughout, Washington is a genuine star; drama jumps from his square-cut features. His acting here . . . is appealing, even if it's all show." *TV Guide* felt that for the first time he had a chance to show "a charming, playful side." Even *New York*, which hadn't been thrilled by the film, had to concede that Denzel played the "very responsible, a bit square" Demterius "with dignity and force." In other words, he'd notched up yet another triumph, one that took away the bad taste of his last part. Maybe not on the scale of *Cry Freedom* or *Glory*—this was, after all, a smaller, *artier* film—but another marvelous display of acting nonetheless. He'd done something much harder than make a hero out of a man of genius, like Bleek, or a freedom fighter like Biko. He'd found the magic in the ordinary man, the way someone good and decent, an everyday person, could be remarkable. To be fair, some of that was due to the writing, but it was Denzel who brought him to life, the mixture of shyness and boldness, the boy and the man in one package. It helped that, in ways, the qualities that made Demetrius so good, so appealing, were a natural part of Denzel himself. The earnestness, the desire to work, to make something of himself; that wasn't acting, that was a mirror. But, generally, those have been uninteresting qualities on the screen, and, since Jimmy Stewart, largely out of fashion. To make an audience root for that little man—which Demetrius was, in the larger scheme going on around him—to make him living and vibrant, and capable of rising above the circumstances that threatened to consume him—that was the gift Denzel brought to this movie. And which made his performance so outstanding, stardom in quality as well as name. That little word—star—was being bandied around more and more often now in connection with his name.

Whereas the Denzel Washington of *Ricochet* had been a very physical presence, bulging biceps and full of action, the Denzel of *Mississippi Masala* was a completely different person. He even *looked* different—scrawnier to the point of thinness, shyer, younger. But that was part of his magic as an actor. He had the ability to transform himself into what the role needed. He wasn't a star in the traditional sense, who had the same face and same voice in a number of different parts. He was a real actor, one who totally submerged himself in his character. It was something he'd done from the days of his first stage appearances, a gift he used wisely and well. It made him something special, but it also raised the question: who exactly was Denzel Washington?

The answer, of course, was simple. Denzel was the real man. The people he played onscreen were the fictions, the masks he raised to face the world. Denzel was the family man whose wife had just had twins, Malcolm and Olivia, giving them a total of four children. He was the narrator of *Anansi*, a

West Indian childrens' tale (spoken in his Quinn accent) that was distributed on audio and video. He was many things, an actor, an African-American, a husband, and a father.

And soon, for almost a year and a half, he'd become someone else again. It was all a part of the job.

EIGHT

Denzel had first come to critical attention playing Malcolm X on stage. Even then he knew that someday he'd end up playing the man onscreen.

So when he was offered the opportunity, there was never a possibility he'd turn it down. He'd dreamed of this, and been working toward being able to handle this role for years. Playing one of the great black (and Black Muslim) leaders was nothing less than the chance of a lifetime.

However, even reaching the stage where the film could be made was a long and tortuous road. Originally, white Canadian Norman Jewison, a man with an enviable track record (*In the Heat of the Night, The Thomas Crown Affair*) was slated to be the director (with Denzel in the title role), working from a script by Charles Fuller, an established black playwright.

Spike Lee was insistent, though, that no white man could adequately tell Malcolm's story. And he was probably right. As he made more and more noise on the topic, eventually Warner Brothers gave way, and the project became Lee's.

That however, wasn't quite enough for him. Virtually the only holdover from Jewison's work was Denzel's casting. Lee insisted on rewriting the entire script, which caused conflict within the black community, as Amiri Baraka, a spokesman for the United Front to Preserve the Legacy of Malcolm X (and a respected poet and playwright in his own right), denounced Lee, asserting that he would "trash" the story of Malcolm's life "to make middle-class Negroes sleep easier."

Lee's reaction was quite pointed: "This film . . . is going to be *my* vision of Malcolm X," he replied, although he did base his screenplay on an earlier version, by James Baldwin and Arnold Perl.

And that was exactly what he gave people. With a budget of twenty-eight million dollars, he intended to make the first black epic motion picture. Moreover, he succeeded.

Any film concerning Malcolm X couldn't help but be political. Still, in its opening sequence, Lee unabashedly announced his position with a video of the beating of Rodney King and an American flag burning into an X. No one would be sleeping more easily after this.

For Denzel, playing Malcolm meant a great deal

of preparation. He was used to that, of course; it was part of his routine for every production he was involved in. For this, though, he took it two steps further. He watched hours and hours of videotape, talked to Malcolm's friends and relatives, spent days poring over the man's FBI and prison records, and attended Fruit of Islam extra classes. To be convincing in one of the movie's early sequences, he even learned to dance the Lindy Hop.

He fasted, and for most of the shooting period, followed the Muslim teaching of eating only one meal a day. More than anything, he tried to establish a spiritual connection between himself and his character.

Denzel appeared in virtually every scene of the film. Even for an actor of his ability, someone who, without doubt, had become a major figure of the screen, it was a very heavy, exhausting weight to carry. *Malcolm X* depended completely upon him. If he was convincing, if he *was* Malcolm, it could succeed. Anything less would be total failure.

It was a stirring story, of a man's growth, spiritually and emotionally, coming to maturity and realizing his potential. That man just happened to be black.

He was born Malcolm Little, the son of a preacher and his wife. The Reverend Little was outspoken for his time, preaching a return to Africa for blacks. He was not afraid of the white men, the

Klansmen who rode around his rural Nebraska home.

His wife was a light-skinned woman, still carrying the legacy of a white man raping her ancestor. She wanted her children to be dark, to be proud of their color.

However much the Klan or other white groups harassed them, burned them out of houses, the Littles remained strong. At least, until the Reverend's murder. Officially, it was suicide, but no man was capable of caving in the back of his own skull, and then lying on the streetcar tracks.

The authorities didn't even give Mrs. Little a chance to raise her own children. Declaring them delinquents, they were taken away from her. The family was broken up, to be raised in foster homes.

Malcolm was a bright boy, one of the quickest in his class. But in the thirties, to be black and poor—no matter how intelligent—was more or less a guarantee of a lifetime of menial work.

By the time he was grown, Malcolm Little was living in Boston's Roxbury section, working as a waiter on the railroad, and trying to be as white as possible. His hair was already red, and now he conked it with a mixture of lye, soap, and egg to make it lie flat and look more "white." With his pal Shorty (Spike Lee), he dressed in the latest zoot suits, and went dancing.

It was at a dance that he met Sofia, a white girl. Before too long they were an established couple, and Malcolm ditched his black girlfriend.

On a trip to Harlem, he ended up in a bar fight, which brought him to the attention of a gangster, West Indian Archer. Soon Malcolm was working for him as a numbers runner, taking drugs, living a completely dissolute life as Sofia came down to join him.

Finally he and Archer had a disagreement over a numbers wager—Malcolm claimed he'd won, Archer never recalled the bet—and he and Sofia had to run back to Boston, fearing for their lives.

Living on Harvard Square, they planned a life of crime. But on the very first job, they were caught, ratted on by an accomplice.

Jail was what changed Malcolm, although at first it seemed like it wouldn't, as he spent endless days in solitary confinement for defiance—refusing to read off his number to the guards.

He was approached by another prisoner, Baines, a strong, spiritual man, who tried to talk to him about the Nation of Islam and the teachings of its leader, Elijah Muhammad. It took quite a while for the words to sink into Malcolm's mind, but once they did, he proved to be an enthusiastic and remarkably adept convert to the cause.

After Baines was released, he went to work for the Nation, and promised Malcolm a place there when he got out. Which was how Malcolm ended up meeting Elijah Muhammad (Al Freeman, Jr.) and becoming his disciple.

It quickly became clear that Malcolm, who was now Malcolm X, having dropped Little as a name given by the white slavemasters, was a gifted preacher. Before long, he was the minister of his own mosque in Harlem, rapidly rising in the ranks of the Nation of Islam.

He'd been introduced to Betty Saunders, a nurse and Muslim woman, who'd already decided she wanted to marry him. But one of their early dates was disrupted when a messenger brought the news that a Muslim man had been beaten by the police.

Malcolm wasted no time. He marshaled his men and marched to the precinct house, demanding to see the victim. Outside, the ranks of disciplined black men waited.

Malcolm got to see the man, and insisted on an ambulance for him, then took his people to the hospital, gathering a large, orderly crowd along the way. Only when the doctor offered an assurance that the man would be fine did he disperse his people. It was an awesome display of the power Malcolm X had at his command.

It was enough for Elijah Muhammad, who promoted him to National Minister, with a brief to travel and set up temples all over the country.

Malcolm married Betty, but they were rarely together. He was all too often away from home, and even when he was there, business occupied his time. The children they had, all girls, hardly saw their father.

But some within the Nation of Islam, including Baines, were jealous of the power and attention Malcolm was getting. He was on television, the front page of the newspapers. He'd become a political force within the country, a widely recognized name. So they tried to poison Elijah Muhammad's mind against Malcolm.

The turning point came with the assassination of John F. Kennedy in 1963. Asked to comment on it, Malcolm said that he saw it as a reflection of white violence in America, the chickens come home to roost. His leader wasn't happy with his statement. From telling the truth about the black position in America, he'd decided to become a little conciliatory, and Malcolm's statement had been divisive. Malcolm was ordered not to speak in public for ninety days.

Meanwhile, a scandal concerning the leader had broken. It was alleged that he'd fathered children with a couple of his female disciples. Malcolm investigated, met the women, and saw the babies. Elijah Muhammad himself even admitted it in a private interview with Malcolm.

For Malcolm, that had to be the end. He broke away from the Nation of Islam and its hypocrisies. When he'd spoken at their meetings, he'd been following their teachings. Now he'd follow his own mind. He would reconcile with other black leaders, put the past behind him. He had no hatred of whites as such. He wanted an America where everybody could live as equal human beings. But first he wanted the black man to rise, to become proud.

The Nation of Islam hadn't taken his defection lying down. There were constant threats on his life, late-night anonymous phone calls that terrified Betty. But Malcolm would carry on doing what he needed to do.

What he needed first was a spiritual cleansing. So he made the pilgrimage every Muslim is supposed to make in his lifetime, to the holy city of Mecca, where he mixed with Muslims of every race and color, who had all come together for one purpose.

He came home a stronger man, prepared for the future, whatever it might bring. He continued to speak, continued to be a political force. And the threats still came, culminating in a firebomb thrown through the window of his house that just missed killing him and his family.

He went into hiding, staying at the Hilton. He felt he was safe, but people—including the authorities—knew precisely where he was. He had a speaking engagement lined up, at the Audubon Ballroom, and he wasn't going to miss it, no matter how dangerous it might be. Nor would he allow his followers to search those attending. Black had to trust black. It was the only way.

It should have been the only way. But as Malcolm began to speak, in full view of his wife and daughters, he was gunned down by black assassins. At thirty-nine, Malcolm X was dead. But his message would live on.

The film had been born in controversy, and that never went away. By the time Lee was in the middle of editing, he was five million dollars over budget, and the film's guarantor threatened to close production. Warner Brothers refused to pay the extra money, which led Lee to charge them with racism, an assertion that was vocally backed by Denzel. ". . . That's par for the course," he said. "They come up for white folks. They don't come up for us—ever."

To make the movie happen, Lee took two steps. He contributed two million dollars of his own salary (which was reported as three million dollars), and approached rich blacks for the rest.

There was an immediate outpouring as checks arrived from Bill Cosby, Oprah Winfrey, Magic Johnson, Michael Jordan, Prince, Janet Jackson, and a host of other major talent.

It was a wonderful expression of solidarity, and one which hurriedly spurred Warner Brothers into putting their money back behind the movie again.

But once they saw the film, with its heated opening, there were more troubled discussions. Nor were they happy with its length. Even cut to three hours and twenty-one minutes, it was far longer than the average motion picture. However, that was exactly the point. It was meant to have epic scope, to be an important part of black history.

"Malcolm X was a very complex man," Lee stated in *Jet*. "I believe that his search for truth made him change over and over again and it would be an injustice to his life to take any short-cuts in our film."

Even before its release, the hype surrounding it had grown to massive proportions. All across America, youths were wearing T-shirts and base-ball caps marked with a large X. As Denzel noted to Joe Wood in *Rolling Stone*, ". . . people like the fashion. Half the people walking around don't even know that the X has anything to do with Mal-colm X. . . . But that's really got nothing to do with our film. I mean, ain't no X hats in our picture."

For almost a year and a half Denzel had worked on the film. Every day he'd become Malcolm X for a few hours, and although he knew he wasn't re-ally Malcolm, "I believe the same spirit that moved Malcolm can move me. I believe the same God that affected him can affect me."

And, indeed, it seemed as if He had. Denzel's performance was pure fire, every single minute he was on the screen. He sounded like Malcolm. He looked like Malcolm. Most importantly, the audi-ences *believed* he was Malcolm. If, as Lee asserted, "He really captured Malcolm when he played him in the off-Broadway play," here he achieved an intensity that easily eclipsed that performance. The intent, Denzel said, was for "... kids to see how Malcolm was able to turn his life around, to see that Malcolm's solutions changed as he changed. We want kids to say, 'Maybe I can do that, too.'"

He took a single gesture that was uniquely Malcolm's—the placing of the index finger on the temple—and made it his signature for the role. And, as Malcolm the preacher, he drew a great deal from his own father. His sister, Lorice, commented, "His hand gestures and the rhythms of his voice were Daddy's."

Sadly, though, their father had died the year before; he'd never see his son in his great role.

The long filming process was a physical strain for Denzel. Not only did he have to lose—and keep off—weight, he also had to undergo hair dyeing, and the conking that the young Malcolm had found so painful.

"It was a nightmare," he recalled. "I must have had my hair fried thirty times, dyed thirty times, or some kind of patchwork, streaks, tips."

And inevitably, when he was caught up in his work, he'd withdraw from the world around him, gather his emotions and let them loose inside. As Spike Lee commented warily, "Nobody got next to him the day we had to shoot Malcolm's assassination."

Without any doubt, it was the kind of role that

would make Denzel's reputation as an actor. He was already highly thought of, a critical favorite, but this—at least in the black community—was guaranteed to make him into a superstar. The question was, of course, how would whites, who made up most of the Establishment, react to it?

Maybe the most telling indication was that it wasn't voted Best Film, nor did Denzel win Best Actor, in the Academy Awards. *Malcolm X* was a tremendously important film, but it was politically charged, and it was black.

Because of that, it probably never stood a chance.

Still, the movie that opened nationally on November 20, 1992, was a triumph, not only for Denzel, who was charismatic and commanding as Malcolm, but also for Spike Lee.

Lee, who'd said that "everything from *She's Gotta Have It* to *Jungle Fever* was in preparation for the big one," had made his masterpiece, or, as Denzel called it, "the most controversial film of the decade." There'd been plenty to criticize in his earlier work, but in *Malcolm X* he never put a foot wrong. It had passion, anger, and plenty of intelligent direction—the cutting from color to black-and-white, for instance, to give the impression of vintage news footage. By the time the film ended, with its montage of shots of the real Malcolm X, the audience had been there, lived the experience, and understood. It had the power. It was strong enough to be inspirational.

Lee avoided the easy trap of trying to make Malcolm into a superman. Under it all, he remained a human being, given to accusations, and rage; he wasn't someone who was about to turn the other cheek, just to be slapped again.

But a lot of the critics didn't go away impressed. Many were turned off by what *Time* categorized as a "storm of tumult and hype." While admitting that Lee was "a logo maker of genius" (a reference to the X-wear that seemed to be everywhere), the reviewer felt that "the big surprise about *Malcolm X* is how ordinary it is." Although it was "lavish," and conceding it looked "twice as expensive and expansive" as its budget, it was "way-too-long" and raised "Malcolm's importance until the vital historical content is obscured." Moreover, it committed a greater sin of portraying Malcolm "less as a flamethrower of incendiary rhetoric than as a victim," concluding that the film was "tepid melodrama."

Video found it riddled with "self-indulgence," but admitted that although the "sprawling epic sometimes lacks focus, it's still a striking testament to the electrifying power of ideas."

New Statesman & Society knew that the film stood under "a leaden weight of exorbitant anticipation," and that to live up to that would be almost impossible. Even so, the critic was surprised that the film was "far closer to Hollywood aesthetics than expected," with a "sometimes arid sense of hagiography," concluding that "There's no denying that *Malcolm X* is immensely powerful, or to use a more damning word, compelling—which tends to mean that a film is essentially dull but you don't realize it at the time," and was "Hamstrung by its own seriousness and intelligence."

Commentary was more succinct, calling it "a big letdown, both as entertainment and as politics. Often visually stunning and fun to listen to . . . as a whole *Malcolm X* is leaden and painfully didactic." Acknowledging that "this is not real life, it is legend," the reviewer pointed out "Lee's determination to send a message to his viewers—young black viewers."

The Progressive also found fault with the pacing of the film, believing too much time was devoted to the earlier phases of the life, and "As a result, the last two years of Malcolm's life—in which he consolidated his role as a national figure—fly by as a blur." The overall effect was "like watching assembly-line production." The critic wasn't surprised to find the film sexist (a charge that had been leveled at Lee before), but was struck more at how the film "slides over the source of Malcolm's prominence as a figure in American life," the effect of which was to "depoliticize a historical figure whose claim on public attention was his political insurgency."

Commonweal, too, found problems with some of the film, although the reviewer did gush that "Lee has taken just measure of the story and has given it the sweep . . . and the sense of the epic it must have to register as entertainment, much less art." Indeed, it was only when Malcolm became an orator that "Lee and the movie run into trouble." Or, to put it more simply, during the first part of the film "we are inside his consciousness . . . But once Malcolm Little becomes Malcolm X, we are outside his consciousness."

The *National Review*, however, was far more complimentary. The writer knew that Lee had skated over some of Malcolm's political problems, but truly did feel that he "has made a genuine contribution to Contemporary American Cinema" with "a genuine piece of filmmaking . . . and devilishly good acting."

But what about Denzel's part in this? Although the critics had been all too quick—rightly or wrongly—to pounce on the faults within the movie, what of him? This was, after all, his role of a lifetime. Had to lived up to it?

The *National Review* found him to be "the ideal interpreter . . . Washington manages to be playful and formidable, touching and terrifying, without once seeming excessive in a role that must have been an invitation to excess."

Commonweal, too, was convinced by Denzel, saying that in the movie's first third, ". . . Washington is Clark Gable come again . . . [he] has a knack, whenever his character is in danger or is about to strike out, of keeping his head very still and letting his eyes go vacant." And later, as X "Washington continues to score as he conveys his character's rage with an amused iciness that seems to amplify the anger rather than mitigate it."

New Statesman & Society praised his "charismatic sobriety," which "transcends mere photo-imitation of his model," and *Video* also termed him "charismatic," saying that he "couldn't be better," with a "quiet intensity."

To many people, particularly the younger generation that picked up on the X shirts and caps, Malcolm was little more than a figure from history. To them he might as well have been from the 1760s, instead of the 1960s. His words, and what he meant, not only to a people, but to an entire country, were little more than quotes in schoolbooks. The myth of Malcolm X, such as it was, overshadowed the person.

Denzel brought him out into the light. He took the myth and put flesh and bones on it, clothed it, made it into a living, speaking thing. The charisma that had informed all his performances thus far was perfect for the role of such a truly charismatic leader. When Denzel, as Malcolm, marched his men to the precinct house, then on to the hospital, the entire group perfectly disciplined, there was never any doubt that it had happened that way. The character and the performance simply had that much power. With one look he was capable of communicating the compassion, the rage, the thoughtfulness of Malcolm. But it was in his speeches, the words lifted from Malcolm's texts, that actor and character truly became one. As Denzel had noted, he felt it happening, but in the theater its impact was stunning. Denzel no longer existed; there was simply Malcolm, filling the screen, as alive as he had been thirty years earlier, as vibrant and questing. This wasn't myth. This was *real*. Maybe it had been a black thing, but this time around you didn't have to be black to understand the message. What Denzel achieved was nothing short of stunning.

Beyond any doubt, it was a performance worthy of a number of awards, and while they evaded the movie, they soon started to flow to Denzel. At the Chicago Film Critics Awards, he was voted Best Actor for the role. The Berlin Film Festival gave him their Silver Bear Award for the performance. But almost as might have been expected, although Denzel was nominated as Best Actor in both the Golden Globe and Academy Awards, neither trophy came to him.

He lost out on the Oscar for Best Actor to Al Pacino in *Scent of a Woman*. Although many thought Denzel should have won, he wasn't too surprised by the decision.

"I didn't lose any sleep before or after," he said later. "... It's the truth. I want to be the best actor in the world. I was taught that's what you're supposed to try to be—the best. The best is not quantified by four thousand six hundred people voting."

He knew he'd given his all to the role, that he'd become one with Malcolm for the length of shooting. He couldn't have done any more, or done it any better. In his own mind he'd been the best. What the Academy chose to think was dictated by a number of other factors. The fact was that Denzel had absolutely nothing to apologize for. His work had been nothing less than marvelous, from start to finish.

The attention and overwhelming praise Denzel received for his portrayal served to make him one of *People*'s "Twenty-five Most Intriguing People" of 1992, where his pastor, Bishop Charles Blake, correctly assessed him as "a plain, unassuming person." And Denzel himself said, "I am not a movie star," although Kate Vernon, who had played Sofia, might have disagreed, finding him "very sexy," and saying that, after her audition with him, "I had to sit down on a chair and collect myself."

Still, regardless of how many awards it did or didn't win, *Malcolm X was* an important film. And because of it, Denzel had mass recognition as a black actor. That was a compliment, but it could also be a dead end of sorts. The very term limited him. He was an actor who was black, and that was a big distinction.

Quite obviously, he needed to look further afield.

NINE

Where could Denzel go from here? By playing Malcolm X he'd reached a pinnacle of sorts, and for the moment there were no higher mountains to climb.

Perhaps that was just as well. He'd spent so long immersed in his character that he needed a real break, something that offered a little light relief and not too much involvement while he let himself resurface.

The film that English actor/director Kenneth Branagh was proposing gave exactly that chance. An adaptation of Shakespeare's *Much Ado About Nothing*, it was already set to star Branagh and his then-wife, Emma Thompson, both wonderful performers, along with Keanu Reeves and Michael Keaton—a remarkably curious mixture. The version of the play that Branagh proposed wasn't exactly traditional, but kept much of the original, frothy spirit. And he offered Denzel the part of the Prince Don Pedro.

It was a minor role, part of the ensemble, but that was fine. Denzel needed a change from carrying the weight of movies on his shoulders. For anyone who'd ever acted on the stage, Shakespeare was the work you aspired to, and Denzel felt no differently than anyone else who'd ever trod the boards.

He could have fun, work with some very interesting talents, and, as a bonus, see Italy, where *Much Ado About Nothing* was due to be filmed.

As a comedy of errors, *Much Ado About Nothing* was a funny, often bawdy piece, a true battle of the sexes.

On their way home from the wars, the Prince and his band stopped to rest at a friend's house, where Beatrice (Emma Thompson) lived.

It wasn't long before Beatrice and Benedick (Branagh) were verbally sparring, as they always did when they met. The others knew they were in love, but it was something they couldn't admit to themselves.

One of the Prince's other traveling companions, Claudio (Robert Sean Leonard) was telling his colleagues of his love for another daughter of the house, Hero (Kate Beckinsale). The Prince offered to act as his messenger, wooing her on his behalf.

It looked as if romance was thoroughly in the air—except for Don John (Keanu Reeves), the

Prince's bastard brother, who'd been forced to abandon his own campaign for the throne and pledge allegiance to the Prince. What he wanted was revenge.

His first opportunity came at that evening's party, when he told Claudio that the Prince really wanted Hero for himself. But that balloon was burst when the Prince appeared with Hero and gave her hand to Claudio.

All wasn't lost for Don John, though. His servant had established a relationship with Hero's maid, and it was carefully arranged for the Prince and Claudio to see them together in Hero's window that night. It looked as if Hero had been unfaithful.

The next day, at the wedding ceremony, Claudio rejected his bride, who fainted. The royal party left, except for Benedick, who declared his love for Beatrice, wondering what he could do to win her hand. The answer was quick: "Kill Claudio!"

Hero's family and friends knew there was nothing to the charges of infidelity, but decided to let it be known that she'd died of a broken heart. Claudio was devastated, and even more so when his old friend Benedick challenged him to a duel.

Of course, the truth would inevitably come to light. The members of the night watch, under the eyes of Dogberry (Michael Keaton) had apprehended Don John's servant as he boasted about the incident, and brought him before the magistrate, who in turn took him to the Prince. And Don John had mysteriously disappeared.

Claudio, grief-stricken, agreed to do penance, to pray all night at the church, erect a notice there stating that Hero was pure, and, the following day, marry, sight unseen, one of her cousins.

The guests for this second wedding were more somber than they'd been for the first. But when Claudio lifted his new wife's veil he saw . . . Hero! How had it happened? It didn't matter. He was overjoyed.

It was obvious, too, that Beatrice and Benedick would also marry, to keep teasing each other for the rest of their lives.

The reaction of the critics was decidedly mixed. Emma Thompson was universally praised—and her performance truly did sparkle—but many weren't taken with the film itself. *The New Leader* felt "the hilarity always well-drilled, even if it misses a touch of spontaneity," while this version missed the deeper, underlying issues. In the *National Review*, John Simon felt that Branagh's changes to the play made "for less ado and more nothing," but was willing to concede that, in the end, ". . . he does give us a rollickingly extroverted *Much Ado*, quickly converting its sounds of woe into a hey nonny, nonny." *Commonweal* had a similarly mixed opinion, admitting that it wasn't a great Shakespeare film, before continuing, "But it does have what few Shakespeare films, what few movies of *any* sort possess: zest." The *New Republic* had praise for many of the elements, but was forced to sum it up as "a flawed gem. Certainly, regrettably, flawed; still, a gem."

In the *Nation*, however, the writer found few faults, suggesting that Branagh's *Much Ado About Nothing* "at its best reaches a level beyond criticism. It makes you marvel anew at Shakespeare."

One thing the critics did seem to agree on, though, was Denzel's work in the movie. For years he'd received mostly ecstatic praise for his film performances. This time, it seemed, it was his turn to be the subject of the backlash.

While the *Christian Century* deemed his Don Pedro "convincing and weighty," most of the opinions leaned strongly in the other direction. To the *New Leader*, "An aimless easy heartiness, a sort of debonair mist suffuses ... Washington, a transparent disguise of embarrassment," and *Commonweal* felt he offered "a callow performance, more like a warm-up than a finished work."

But by far, the most savage words came from *National Review*'s John Simon, who wondered "What is Denzel Washington, a black Prince of Aragon, doing in such a persuasive period setting?" He wrote about the "technical problem" a black actor had "in a nocturnal torch-lit scene," and the historical probability (or lack thereof) of Don Pedro actually being black.

Simon was willing to concede that "Washington is a fine actor in the right part," then pointed out "... he has no Shakespearian training, as he painfully demonstrated in the title part of the New York Shakespeare Festival's hapless *Richard III*. Moreover, his idea of sounding genteel makes him talk with a finishing school accent; he is also too young for the part and lacks royal bearing.''

Somehow, one was forced to wonder how much of this venom was directed at Denzel's performance in the movie, and how much at the man himself. After all, there was no reason why a black actor should not play Don Pedro. Shakespeare might never have specified it, the way, say, he'd made Othello black, but it was the quality of the acting, not the color of the skin, that mattered. And the quality of Denzel's acting had never been in any doubt. Maybe he didn't shine here quite as brightly as he had in other films, but he still managed to bring a regal, playful quality to the part, exactly the tenor it needed. He had the bearing of a leader, and the relaxed air of a man on his way home, with war now behind him and the kingdom settled—in other words, many of the things the critics were now roasting him for. Nor was there the need to declaim like a classical actor. This was film, not stage; no one had to play to the gallery. What Denzel, and the others, did was to speak in normal voices, and let the rhythm and poetry of Shakespeare's words dictate the speech—something the Bard would probably have approv if he'd been alive in the nineties.

Maybe the truth was that some of the

found themselves offended that Branagh had made Shakespeare a joy, rather than keeping him a museum piece, and took out their anger on all concerned, particularly Denzel, being the one who stood out most because of his color. Or perhaps it was just his turn to be the one on the receiving end of dire words.

Being in the public eye, it was something that was bound to happen sooner or later. Maybe the greatest surprise about the diatribes was that they had been so long in coming.

Or then again, maybe not.

A lot of people knew Denzel's name—after all, he'd worked enough—and some would recognize his face. But for all the acclaim he'd received, he remained an actor who was slightly removed from the mainstream. His biggest roles had been in pictures that were either very "black" (*Malcolm X, Mo' Better Blues, Mississippi Masala, The Mighty Quinn, Glory*; even *Cry Freedom* could be considered that way), or fairly unsuccessful (*Heart Condition, For Queen and Country, Ricochet*).

He had yet to make that breakthrough to the mass, white audience. If any black actor could do it, it would be him. He possessed charm, looks, poise, and talent. Indisputably, he had the looks and the talent. *Malcolm X* had shown the full range of his power onscreen.

He needed two things to help him up the ladder to superstardom—wider visibility, and a perfect starring vehicle. And after the vacation of *Much Ado About Nothing*, he was ready to begin looking for both.

But first things first. That starring vehicle would have to wait a little while. The audiences in multiplexes needed to become used to him first, which meant a period in co-starring, possibly even supporting, roles. On the surface, it almost looked like a move backward for someone who'd seen his name headlining so many movies. But it made perfect sense.

The offers were already there; now it was time to take them. First as Joe Miller, the lawyer in Jonathan Demme's *Philadelphia*. Demme had swept the Oscars with *The Silence of the Lambs*, and his new film was greatly anticipated, being the first major production to deal with AIDS, a subject that remained touchy (and indelibly associated with gays) to most of America.

But there was also another part, in a movie that also seemed certain to be commercially successful—playing the reporter, Gray Grantham, in Alan Pakula's screen version of John Grisham's bestselling novel *The Pelican Brief*.

It had all the elements of a winner—name recognition, a star who was immensely popular at the box office (Julia Roberts), and, in Pakula, a director who'd made movies that not only brought in money, but also good notices (*All the President's Men, Presumed Innocent*). If Denzel minded playing second banana—although in both cases, they were very strong co-starring roles—he didn't show it.

As both a hardcover and paperback, *The Pelican Brief* had sold remarkably well, and the suspenseful story seemed a natural for a movie.

Julia Roberts played Darby Shaw, a Tulane University law student having an affair with one of her professors, Thomas Callahan (Sam Shepard). When two Supreme Court Justices were assassinated, one of them a man Callahan had known and clerked for, Darby became intrigued. On the surface there was little in common between the two judges, Rosenberg and Jensen. But when Darby researched more deeply, she did find one area where they'd agreed—the environment.

That led her deep into the law library, where she came up with something that neither the FBI nor the CIA had managed—a possible motive for the murders. They'd tentatively identified the killer, a hit man known as Khamel, but they had no idea why he'd been hired.

Darby's essay, which she titled the Pelican Brief, offered a theory. Victor Mattiece, a billionaire industrialist, owned a company that had struck oil off the Louisiana coast. He'd managed to have the state legislature allow him to wreak havoc on the shoreline to bring the oil up—or would have, until he was challenged by a tiny environmental group, which charged that the damage could cause the end of the Louisiana brown pelican.

For the moment things remained tied up in

court. But it seemed very likely that within five years the case would end up being heard by the Supreme Court. And Mattiece, who'd been the single largest contributor to the president's campaign fund, wanted the court stacked so it would decide in his favor, when that time came.

If Darby was right, that meant the ripples of this conspiracy extended well into the White House. She showed the brief to Callahan, who took it with him to Washington when he attended Rosenberg's memorial service.

While there, he showed it to an old friend, another lawyer who'd become the counsel to the FBI's director, Boyles.

Far-fetched as it seemed, the brief caused an immediate stir. The FBI wanted to follow up on it, but at the President's behest, they held off. And the President's Chief of Staff, Fletcher Cole, swung into action.

Back in New Orleans, Darby and Callahan had been out for the evening. He insisted he wasn't drunk and that he was fine to drive home. She disagreed. After an argument, she began to walk. In the car, he turned the ignition.

And the car exploded.

When Darby came to, she was sitting in a car with two men who claimed to be New Orleans police detectives. But when she talked to the real cops, they had no record of men with those names. She realized she was in danger, and began to run.

Meanwhile, in D.C., Gray Grantham, an investigative reporter with the *Washington Herald,* started to get calls from a man who went by the alias Garcia, who claimed to have information about the murders. He wanted to pass it on, but he was scared. Grantham was able to discover that he'd been calling from a phone booth, and staked it out. When Garcia called again, he answered on his mobile phone, all the time snapping photographs of the man. He was able to figure out that Garcia was a lawyer, but he wasn't able to follow him to see where he worked.

Darby was in a hotel, but not safe. She foiled one attempt to kidnap and silence her, then holed up in another hotel, where she was kept under surveillance. She contacted Callahan's lawyer friend with the FBI, who offered her protection, which she refused—for all she knew, the men trying to kill her could have been with that agency. She promised to contact him when he arrived in New Orleans for Callahan's funeral.

Then she saw Grantham (Denzel) interviewed on television, and phoned him. She wouldn't tell him much, giving a false name, and mentioning the Pelican Brief, a name that meant nothing to him. By now Garcia had backed off, leaving him with nothing.

What Darby didn't realize was that Khamel was back in the country. And this time she was his target.

He was waiting when she contacted the lawyer, killed him, and took his place for the meeting she'd set up. On the banks of the Mississippi, just as he was about kill her in broad daylight in the middle of a crowd, a shot fired, and he fell, dead.

Again, Darby had no choice but to run, this time to New York. She contacted Grantham again, offering some verification of her story. He flew up to meet her.

Over the course of an evening she laid out the entire conspiracy for him. He fitted in what little he knew of Garcia. They needed evidence for the *Herald* to publish the story, and Garcia was the man to provide it. He needed her help to track the man down, but she refused. She wanted to leave the country.

Grantham's editor wanted to pull him from the assignment. There were no facts, nothing that could be put on paper. But Grantham was able to persuade the man to let him stay with it a little longer.

At his cabin for the weekend, Gray was disturbed by dogs barking. Going out to investigate, he found Darby. She hadn't gone abroad after all; that was just a ruse.

For now, they were both on the run.

Through a process of elimination, they were able to work out where Garcia worked. That narrowed things down a little. After talking to students at Georgetown Law School who'd clerked at the firm,

they were able to come up with a name for him—
Curtis Morgan.

Their sense of victory was very brief, though.
Curtis Morgan had died the week before, in a mugging.

Grantham visited Morgan's wife. She'd found
nothing strange in his papers, but there was a key
to a safe-deposit box. Posing as the widow, Darby
emptied it the next day, finding a file and a videotape.

Grantham and Darby didn't know a bomb had
been planted in their car, but realized it before
Gray could start the engine. And there were agents
all over the garage where they were parked, waiting to pick them off. It looked like the end of the
road.

Eventually they made it out, and to the *Washington Herald's* office, where they handed over the evidence, including a copy of the memo Morgan/
Garcia had accidentally picked up, which had cost
him his life.

All put together, it was damning. Victor Mattiece
was implicated, as was the law firm, and, most importantly, the White House.

Grantham and Shaw met with FBI Director
Boyles, who offered them protection. Darby had
only one demand—that she be flown out of the
country. This time she really was leaving.

When the story appeared, it sent shock waves
through the government. Mattiece was indicted,

Chief of Staff Cole resigned. Word came down that the President would not be running for reelection. A law student and the Pelican Brief had changed the country, and avenged five deaths.

The Pelican Brief did excellent business, taking in sixty-one million dollars in its first month of release, but it wasn't exactly loved by reviewers. *Entertainment Weekly* felt it had "no emotional core," when it reviewed the video release, which echoed the same magazine's view of the film when it appeared as "a deadening rhythm of snoop, get chased, hide in a hotel room," summing up that "The wheels of justice grind slowly in *The Pelican Brief*. Really slowly." The *Nation* dismissed it as being "cinema as board game." And *Time* felt that audiences went to movies like this "to have the pants scared off us. That doesn't happen in *The Pelican Brief*."

Something that many critics did pick up on, though, was the absence of any sex, not even a kiss, between Gray and Darby. In the book, they became lovers at the end. But in the film, that was very noticeably absent, and the general speculation was that it had been because Denzel was black and Roberts was white. Interracial sex could happen often in real life, but onscreen it remained very much a taboo subject.

The Pelican Brief was always meant to be Julia Roberts's film, her vehicle, and that was exactly the way it turned out. What was far more interesting was the way Denzel approached the character of Grantham. For over half the movie he was there, crucial to the action, but he came across as stolid, businesslike, and quite devoid of personality, more a cipher than a person.

That seemed odd, for if there was one unifying thread to the roles Denzel had played, it was that they were very much alive, sparkling with personality. And Roberts said of him in *Time*, "Denzel is very grounded in who he is and what he's doing and why he's doing it."

But this time he seemed so grounded that he was almost rooted. *Entertainment Weekly* offered a possible reason: "As for Washington, it's doubtful whether there's a smarter leading man working today," before adding, "His role is reactive—Gray mostly responds to the information Darby and others give him—but the actor shuts the doors of his face and gets us wondering how he'll react." That was certainly one explanation. But why employ an actor of his caliber in such a flat role? Simple—like Roberts, he had the ability to draw an audience at the box office, albeit a slightly different one.

Perhaps he gave such a flat reading of Grantham to avoid stealing the picture from Julia Roberts. After all, she was the headliner, and she had picked him for the role of Gray. She was certainly better than adequate, but her performance was hardly incandescent. Without too much effort, Denzel could have been the audience's main memory of *The Pel-*

ican Brief. That wouldn't have seemed too good, and the director might not have allowed it to happen. Technically he might have been the co-star, but there was no doubt whose name was in the bigger, brighter lights.

According to *Entertainment Weekly* he wasn't too happy with the initial advertising for the movie, which featured a blown-up picture of Roberts, with Denzel not particularly prominent in the corner— a discrepancy that didn't reflect his growing stature in the business, and which, really, was little more than an insult to him. He was the co-star, and under the "favored nation" status, was guaranteed equal billing in most areas, which included advertising. So he talked to Warner Brothers, who were putting out the movie. Denzel wouldn't comment on whether he threatened a lawsuit—"Let's say we sat down and we worked it out," was his official statement—but the new poster showed him far more prominently.

As he noted, "I'm marketable now." He was a star who was becoming more recognizable every day, and who was getting roles that would previously have gone to white actors (like the part of Gray Grantham. But he'd earned his stature. "It's not like they're doing me a favor by giving me these roles."

And from here, the only direction he would be moving was up. All the way to the top.

TEN

From the outset, there was no doubt that *Philadelphia* would be a major film. Originally known as *Probable Cause*, it was the first major Hollywood production to deal with AIDS. That alone guaranteed it a great deal of publicity, given that the topic was, and remains, so controversial in the minds of so many. Add to that the fame director Jonathan Demme had won with *The Silence of the Lambs*, and you had one of the most eagerly awaited movies of the decade.

Maybe the biggest question was whether it could live up to all the advance word, and that seemed an impossible task. But Demme had assembled a topflight cast, and arranged for many of the country's leading musicians (Bruce Springsteen, Neil Young, etc.) to be on the sound track. If it failed, it wouldn't be for the lack of talent involved in the project.

Definitely it was a bold move for Tom Hanks to play Andrew Beckett, the young lawyer stricken with the disease. To be fair, he wasn't a major sex symbol whose career could be ruined by playing a gay man. But his box-office success had been achieved mostly by taking on comedic roles (*Bonfire of the Vanities* being a big exception; and that was a flop), and there was nothing remotely farcical about this.

Denzel knew Hanks's work from his comedies, but soon gained respect for him in a dramatic role. "... I'm even more impressed with what a good dramatic actor he is," he said. "I saw his dedication—how focused and disciplined he was."

Certainly, for Hanks it was a tremendous feat. Over the course of the film, he had to become more and more gaunt, which meant losing more and more weight. But he managed it.

Denzel knew that any project of Demme's meant quality, and he was a director he wanted to work with. "Then I read the script," he told *Jet*, "and saw how wonderful it was and how good Joe's part was and how important the subject matter was."

Miller had been written as a *white* part—the original script made no mention of his being black. But neither Denzel nor Demme wanted to let something as minor as that get in the way of working together.

"I've always wanted to work with this amazing actor," Demme told *Go*. "Then I'm doing this white-bread *Philadelphia*. The next thing I know, I'm on the phone to Denzel Washington. But this part is not African-American. I said, 'You've read the script—do you think we'd have to make any adjustments in a character who is in theory written as a European person?' Denzel said, 'No. Do you?' I said, 'No. I don't.' Then I got excited. It never wore off."

As always, Denzel undertook plenty of research to become Miller. He spent time in court, hearing the ebb and flow of lawsuits coming to trial. More than that, he got to know some personal injury lawyers (his character's speciality), and studied them and the way they worked. It stood him in good stead. By the time filming began, he knew precisely what he wanted to achieve, someone who was a strong lawyer, but with a touch of hustler, and, underneath, startlingly conservative. Indeed, Denzel got so much under Miller's skin that he was able to add a few lines of dialogue that really helped illuminate the character—some of the kitchen scene, where Miller ranted against gays to his wife, came from Denzel's improvisation.

Although Hanks received top billing, Denzel was, to all intents and purposes, the co-star. His character, Joe Miller, was as much in the foreground as Andrew Beckett—indeed, for most of the courtroom scenes, even more so.

Andrew Beckett was a rising star in his Philadelphia law firm. An associate, he'd just achieved a big victory in a judge's chambers, beating Joe Miller in an important suit.

His bosses, the partners, were all impressed by his work, ability, and potential. They'd just taken on a new client, and Beckett was made senior associate assigned to look after the case.

But what Andrew hadn't told them was that he was already suffering from AIDS. A gay man, he'd contracted the HIV virus, which had become AIDS, and which was slowly decimating his immune system.

For the moment the only outward sign was a tiny lesion—Kaposi's syndrome—on his forehead. When one of the partners asked about it, Beckett concocted a tale about a squash injury.

But the partner had seen this type of blemish before, in Washington. He knew full well what it was. And though Beckett had just been promoted, his fate was already sealed.

The new responsibility brought even longer working hours, and much more stress, which his weakened body didn't handle well. His life partner (Antonio Banderas) had to take him to the hospital, but Beckett returned home to work. The lesions were more prominent, forcing Beckett to cover them with makeup.

The night before the deadline for filing the brief on the case, he completed it, and left it on his desk.

The next day brought a frantic call. The brief had vanished. Nor was it on the hard drive of his computer. It was as if it had never existed. Finally, just in time, it was found—in the library.

It looked as if Beckett had made a mistake, something that could almost have been a major error. And the firm couldn't stand for that. Beckett was fired.

But he knew he'd done his job, and done it well. He suspected the real reason behind his dismissal, and the conspiracy that caused it, was the fact that he had AIDS.

He talked to a number of lawyers, but none was willing to take on his case of wrongful termination. Finally he arrived in Joe Miller's office.

At first Miller didn't even remember him. The smart, confident Beckett had gone, replaced by someone who'd lost his hair, and looked ill.

Miller had built up a good practice as a personal injury attorney, giving out his card to all and advertising widely on television. If he was something of an ambulance chaser, at least he was dedicated.

His home life was good. He and his wife had just had their first child, a girl, whom he adored, and was determined to protect.

So when Beckett announced he had AIDS, Miller was squirming in his seat. There was no way he wanted to be associated with this; he didn't even want the man in his office, breathing the same air, as if he could catch the disease.

He turned the case down.

The next time Miller encountered Beckett was in the law library, when a librarian, understanding what was wrong, asked Beckett if he wouldn't be more comfortable somewhere else. The reply was terse, but proud.

Miller talked to him. He still hadn't found an attorney to represent him, so he was researching the precedents himself. After all, Beckett was still a lawyer, even if he was unemployed.

Miller finally agreed to become Beckett's counsel. Not out of any sympathy or empathy, but on legal principle. If the man had been discriminated against, he deserved representation, and his day in court. But it wasn't going to be easy for him. Miller had to overcome his own homophobia, his instinctive distaste of gays, and see Beckett as a person, not a stereotype.

The firm, of course, had hoped that Beckett would already be dead by the time the case came to trial. It was bad enough that their name was being dragged through the mud this way. If they lost, it would mean the end of years of hard work.

But Beckett, more through sheer determination than anything else, held on, and took his place in the courtroom. He'd assisted Miller in his research, and discovered evidence that was potentially damning to his former employers.

And in turn, getting to know him, Miller had begun to understand and respect him. He'd been forced to change his way of thinking, if only a little, and to open his mind.

Miller proved to be the perfect lawyer for Beckett. He was far from the corporate, stodgy person the law firm was using. His tactics were occasionally flamboyant. Sometimes he put himself out on a dangerous limb, or asked that things be explained to him as if he were a six-year-old—a favorite phrase—stated in simple English the jury could understand. He wanted to show that he was a man of the people.

For a while it seemed as if it could go either way. What Miller brought to light wasn't especially remarkable, until he brought a woman to the stand. She, too, was dying of AIDS, having been infected through the transfusion of tainted blood. She'd worked with one of the partners in Washington. He'd been aware of her condition, and done his best to avoid her. At the time, her lesions of Kaposi's syndrome had been very visible. He would have known what they were.

Eventually it came time for Beckett to take the stand himself. It was here that Miller pulled his most effective trick. The lesions on his face were barely visible now. But earlier, they'd been quite plain, and even the makeup he'd worn couldn't disguise them. Now the larger lesions were on his chest. Miller had him remove his shirt, and show his emaciated frame. The purple blotches were clearly visible to anybody.

It was a shock tactic, showboating, true Perry Mason stuff, but it was enough to win the case, and everybody knew it. From there it was a slow downhill glide to the jury's decision, something that was confirmed when one of the partners broke down and admitted the awful way he'd tormented a gay shipmate when he was in the Navy.

But Beckett was weakening all the time. He was in the hospital, on oxygen, when Miller came by to congratulate him on their win. The family was gathered around, celebrating.

In the end, though, the victory was Pyrrhic. Andy Beckett died during the night. He'd won a right for a lot of people who'd follow him, but his personal battle had ended.

It was a powerful story, handled with careful tenderness. In lesser hands, it could easily have become maudlin or saccharine, but Demme kept it far away from that, while still allowing it to be very human, letting us feel for Beckett, and see the changes that happened in Miller.

Needless to say, it attracted the attention of virtually every movie critic in America. Although many praised it, there were more than a few who felt it didn't go far enough in portraying the gay lifestyle, watering that element down to be acceptable for Middle America, or as *Entertainment Weekly* wrote, it "turns out to be a scattershot liberal message movie, one that ties itself in knots trying to render its subject matter acceptable to a mass audience." *Maclean's* agreed with that, sensing that it was "careful not to inflame," but did point out that it was the "first [film] devoted to the issue of intolerance toward homosexuals," adding that it had "tremendous emotional resonance." Which was certainly true. It stayed with the viewer long after the closing titles had faded. While the *New Republic* didn't walk away totally convinced by *Philadelphia*, it did admit that the movie was "patently genuine," while adding that "the producers seem to have lost their senses at the end of the film"—a montage of home movies of Andrew.

Cosmopolitan termed it a "splendid, profoundly stirring drama . . . that restores honor to Hollywood," concluding that it was "a triumphant vehicle for brotherly love."

And then, of course, there were those who weren't at all happy with it. The *Christian Century* called it "a cautious, carefully packaged combination of two made-for-TV genres," not so much an entertainment as "a didactic film on a sensitive topic," which had "the mark of a carefully considered marketing strategy." And the *Nation*, in a very unkind review, summed up the script as being of "sub-Neanderthal finesse."

Perhaps the most interesting area, though, was raised in Andrew Sullivan's essay in the *New Re-*

public, where he put forward the theory that the movie was "directed at black America. From its black co-star, Denzel Washington, to its hype in the black press, to a number of critical black-on-black scenes, it was an aggressively black, middle-class film."

Was that true? If it was, certainly not many writers noticed the phenomenon, although the *Christian Century* did add "It's an interesting touch that Demme has an African-American embody the mainline audience's uneasiness over the gay lifestyle." But Sullivan did raise another point that rang very true.

"[*Philadelphia*] brazenly took a black, straight movie icon and made him grapple with a gay man. Denzel Washington's role for this reason took far more social bravery than Hank's."

In other words, it was less stigmatizing to play a gay man than to play a homophobe. And perhaps that was true. One thing the film certainly did was make Denzel confront his own thoughts on homosexuality and AIDS, and to realize that deep down, like many males, he might harbor a smidgen of prejudice.

"I think so. I . . . think so," he said. "Because I didn't think I was [prejudiced] at all. I said, in general, 'I have no problem with homosexuals, and I want to do everything I can to end AIDS . . .' I think that, much like the character—I don't think I'm like the character, first of all—but I think I got a chance to vent certain frustrations, maybe. It was a good education."

It wasn't an easy truth to face, particularly for someone who has been on the receiving end of bigotry himself. But it was a measure of the man he was that he *could* admit it to himself, then work it through in his mind, and be willing to talk about it in public.

Hanks was singled out and showered with praise for his work in the film. But so, too, was Denzel. Together, *Cosmopolitan* felt, they "will reduce you to tears," pointing out that Denzel was "a magnetic, disturbing presence." To the *New Republic* "Washington gives his best performance since *Glory*, seeming to grow before our eyes."

And *Los Angeles* raved about his work in the film: ". . . you want to see great acting, my choice here is Denzel Washington. . . . It was once thought an almost scientific impossibility that Washington could top his performance as the race-war pushing Malcolm X, but here he seems to redefine intensity and passion," or, as *Entertainment Weekly* offered as a slightly backhanded compliment, Denzel gave "an almost generically charismatic performance." Hanks might have been commanding, but it was Denzel who carried the humanity in the film. A courtroom lawyer needed some charisma, if he were to score points with a jury, but Denzel left them transfixed, a mixture of humor, man-of-the-people folksiness, all topped with a very thick veneer of authority. He brought to Joe Miller a warmth, and made him a person who understood that life—the start and the end of it—could touch him. If Beckett was the soul of *Philadelphia*, then Miller was its beating heart. The role served to reinforce in the minds of audiences and critics just what a towering actor Denzel had become. There weren't many anywhere who had the ability to do what he did, to leave themselves outside the soundstage and enter the set as the person they were portraying. That was more than just talent; it was a rare gift. Equally rare was the range that Denzel could show. He was as convincing playing Miller as he was playing Demetrius (in *Mississippi Masala*) or Malcolm X. The man knew no bounds, that was becoming more and more obvious. And it hadn't turned him into a prima donna. He was a professional, on time every day, fully prepared, giving his all. Joe Miller was his all, and excellent it had been. He'd made the film move, pushed it along with the force of his personality.

But it was Hanks's bravura performance that would go on to win him the 1993 Acadamy Award for Best Actor, a very justifiable reward. While Denzel didn't walk away with any trophies of his own for the film, he'd achieved something very necessary for his career—major acceptance by a white audience.

Commercially, the movie was a smash, taking in over eighty million dollars in its first month of release alone. Which meant that Denzel was widely seen and noted. Not that he hadn't been before, as Malcolm X, but this was a *white* film, and that made a world of difference.

He'd moved well beyond the plateau of being a black star, the Sidney Poitier of his era, and now he was taking long strides toward being a top American star in his own right.

It was time. To a certain extent, attitudes were changing. White youth had made heroes out of black musical performers and athletes. Perhaps there really was a new sense of social acceptance.

And if any black actor stood a chance of being a pinup to whites, it was Denzel. There was simply no denying that he was good-looking.

"I don't dwell on that," he told *Ebony* in 1995. "No, it doesn't have anything to do with me. That's just what people might say about me; that's not who I am."

Of course, having his picture on peoples' walls was hardly his aim in life. He wanted acceptance for his acting ability, not an inherited arrangement of flesh and bone. Nor, as a happily married man with four children, was he interested in adulation from women, of whatever color. Although, as he cryptically told Barbara Walters on national television, he had been tempted, and implied that he might have fallen.

If he had, it was very briefly. Denzel didn't offer any more details on the program, and no more were forthcoming later. The tabloids, usually in a feeding frenzy over a remark like that, offered nothing by way of evidence. Whatever indiscretion may have happened had presumably been dealt with privately, at home, rather than in the public eye. He and Pauletta had taken care of things.

One thing was certain, and that was that they weren't about to split up. They'd been together long enough to weather one storm, and that was precisely what they did.

His family remained his rock, and that wasn't going to change. Denzel didn't want them in the spotlight, not his wife, and especially not the kids. As much as he could, he protected them from publicity in order to give the family a chance to live as close to an ordinary life as possible. Every Sunday all six of them went to church. The free time Denzel had between movies was spent with them, rather than with the Hollywood social scene. That kind of life never attracted him.

"He once said to me that he loved having the kids and the wife because it gave him a reason to be working," Matthew Broderick said. "It was like he had something that gave him a focus."

And Denzel's focus remains firmly on his family. His idea of a good time is to enjoy a quiet dinner with Pauletta or to coach his kids' Little League team or basketball, which he has done as much as his time has allowed. It's something he loves to do, as he admitted. "I love it more . . . more than the acting. I do. I *do*. I love it more than the acting. I swear. I do."

But sometimes having Denzel Washington as your coach can be a drawback. On one occasion it caused an accident at the corner of Beverly and Gardner in Los Angeles. Denzel had let his temper get away from him after his son's basketball team had narrowly lost a game. He wasn't angry at his son—far from it—but at the officials, who, he believed, had singled him and his team out for special treatment because of who he was.

"I wouldn't have been so pissed off if we weren't getting robbed by the referees, but we were getting robbed because I was Denzel Washington. I was explaining to my son that sometimes you can do everything the right way and not be treated fair. And I was explaining this to John David as I went through a light."

Doing everything the right way could almost have been Denzel's motto. Apart from the one slip he hinted at when talking to Barbara Walters, that is how he has lived his life. No shortcuts to the top, no series of women on his arm. Just solid work, and a solid family.

He has never reveled in angst, thrown tantrums in interviews, or tried to hit members of the paparazzi. The phrase might seem out of date, but he's a gentleman, and one who keeps his private and public lives very separate.

One passion of Denzel's that success has not

been able to quench is travel. After completing a film, he and Pauletta—accompanied by the kids, if school is out—often take trips, to the Caribbean, Africa, Europe, wherever strikes their fancy. It's a luxury, to be sure, but an indulgence he can afford, and one that also doubles as a remarkable education for the children.

Denzel's innate decency and his dedication to his family have also served to make him something of a role model for young black males in the country. While that's something he hasn't sought—indeed, keeping his family in the background has deliberately deflected the spotlight away from it—it's definitely there. A complicated situation has arisen, where young males, mostly within the black community, are without work and at times without hope. Some of them have children that they don't, and indeed, can't support. In some neighborhoods, the gang has replaced the family as a unit. By his example, Denzel has shown young men that it doesn't need to be that way. No one would claim that everyone who follows his philosophy of working hard is going to succeed to his extent; realistically, very, very few will. What's happening to youth all over America worries him, as it would worry any father. He's lucky; he can insulate his kids from a lot of it. But he knows that others can't, and that something needs to be done. Not quick fixes, but sweeping change that will reach the root causes of poverty and despair, and lower the statistics that show that young black males may spend some time in jail during their lives. If the way Denzel lives his life, his involvement in organizations like the Boys and Girls Clubs of America, can make a difference, he wants to be involved. These are his people, his history.

"So you do what you can," he said. "And you try to make a positive impact where you can."

And in his own understated way he's done just that. By showing that the family can be of the utmost importance in life, by making it his rock, his foundation, he's demonstrating that there are alternatives to the stereotypes of black males often perpetrated by the press.

Whatever story lay behind the snippet he told Barbara Walters, he wasn't going to air his laundry in front of the nation. He'd been imperfect and admitted it. He'd been honest, and made his peace with his wife. They'd been able to put it behind them, and move ahead with their lives.

And moving ahead in his career was what was occupying his mind now.

ELEVEN

Denzel was ready for his run to the big time. After becoming a black star, then a familiar co-star in two extremely popular movies, it was time to establish him as a star in his own right, a star in the white movie world.

For now, that meant a lot of hard work, something he wasn't afraid of—indeed, like most actors, he was very grateful to have the opportunity. Initially it would mean shooting two films back-to-back, then, shortly after, going into a third. At least, since all could be filmed on Hollywood soundstages, he'd be close to home and able to spend some time with his family.

The first was a thriller in an unusual military setting—an atomic submarine, where Denzel took equal billing with the marvelous Gene Hackman, a film Denzel described as "a good balance between substance and action."

And *Crimson Tide* had plenty of substance. Taking its cues from both the Tom Clancy school of techno-thrillers and *The Caine Mutiny*, the intimate setting almost gave it the feel of a filmed stage play. To all intents and purposes there were really only two characters in this film, Captain Frank Ramsey (Hackman), and his new Executive Officer, Lieutenant Commander Ron Hunter (Denzel). The rest were very plainly background figures. The script needed two remarkably strong actors to pull that off convincingly, and it had them.

The USS *Alabama*, one of America's most advanced atomic submarines, was hastily called to duty following an attempted rebellion in the former Soviet Union. The rebels had taken over a nuclear missile site, and were threatening destruction of the United States. The *Alabama*'s mission was, if needed, to fire warheads that would take out the site—a preemptive strike.

Ramsey had seen plenty of combat. He was an old-school Navy man, whose training was in war more than theory. Hunter, on board because the regular Executive Officer was in the hospital, was a different breed of man, trained at Harvard and Annapolis, as much inclined to reflection as blind obedience.

The submarine waited in the cold waters off the Aleutian Islands for its orders, and they were quick to come. Each new message brought the crew closer to the moment of unleashing destruction. But it also brought a Russian submarine close, one thing they definitely didn't need.

Then the order came. Prepare to fire. The Captain was ready for that time. First, though, they had to dive, which blew out the radio, just as another message came through. Only a fraction was clear, but that fragment was confusing—were they to go ahead, or was the last message being counter-manded?

Ramsey was clear about it. In the absence of a new order, the last one stood. Hunter took the opposite view. They *needed* to know what had been said. If they went ahead and launched the missiles, unknowing, they could be responsible for a nuclear holocaust, atomic war.

The two men were at loggerheads. Hunter invoked Naval Regulations, and had the Captain escorted to his quarters, where he was locked in and guarded. It wasn't something he was eager to do, but he had no choice. Now he needed to get the full text of the message.

First, though, he had to do something about the Russian submarine that had reappeared and was attacking. He destroyed it, but its last torpedo still found a target, taking out the *Alabama*'s propulsion. Without any means of moving forward, the huge sub began to sink.

Just before reaching the depth at which water

pressure would crush the hull, engine power was regained. But while the repairs had been going on, some of the officers had released the Captain, and armed themselves. They were going to take the vessel back from what they saw as a mutiny.

With the element of surprise, they succeeded quickly and bloodlessly. Hunter and his followers were locked in the wardroom. Not before Hunter had had the chance to take some countermeasures, though. With the help of a sympathetic NCO, they made their escape. While the Captain was in the weapons room, preparing to fire the missiles, they disarmed the system, and retook the bridge.

When Ramsey returned, it was a standoff. Both groups were armed. The Captain agreed to wait three minutes in the hope that radio communications could be restored, and the full message received. Just in the nick of time, they were. When verified, the message said that the Russian rebels had surrendered. The submarine could stand down. Hunter had been right after all.

In defeat, Ramsey proved magnanimous. At a hearing to determine the events, and what to do about them, he resigned his commission, and recommended Hunter for a command.

It was powerful, dramatic, and with an edge that all too clearly came straight out of the news. But the real tension was in the clash of personalities and ideologies between Hunter and Ramsey. The sparks came from the superb acting by Denzel and

Hackman, a combination that thrilled Denzel.

"I was excited because he is so good," Denzel said. "He's such a fine actor. That gave me extra energy. I always wanted to come prepared. He was always prepared."

Quite naturally, some of the preparation for the part led him to spend a little time on a submarine, an experience he described as "awesome. The destruction and devastation that these atomic subs are capable of is unbelievable."

Appearing in May 1995, it was geared to become one of the early summer blockbusters—which was exactly what it did. As *Rolling Stone* characterized it, *Crimson Tide* wasn't "art, it's jolting summer entertainment," but really, there was nothing wrong with that, as long as it was well done. And this was. As the magazine continued, "it works the audience over with tension and humor." *Entertainment Weekly* called it a "sumptuously exciting undersea thriller that moves forward in quick, propulsive waves." *People* went so far as to term it "an old-fashioned 'guy' movie—no Hugh Grant, no Brad Pitt, no Keanu Reeves, and mostly combat, even if too much of it is verbal." (Interestingly, Pitt, along with Val Kilmer, were among the actors who'd expressed interest in playing Denzel's role).

Oddly, though, neither *Time* nor *Newsweek* could work up much enthusiasm for the film. To the former, it was a "burly, chatty melodrama about the imminence of annihilation," while the latter reduced it to "a war of boorishness vs. sensitivity," quite a reduction of elements, with the characters little more than ciphers "made up by a sweat stylist."

Even *Rolling Stone* granted that the plot ideas were hackneyed; it was the way they were used, and the acting, that made them work, and the critic had nothing but praise for Hackman and Denzel, saying, "They are both terrific, raising a refried film bean into a class act." To *Newsweek*, the best Denzel could do was "bubble with courteous rage." *People* realized that the two leads "carry . . . [the] screenplay on their stalwart backs," while *Time* seemed to find an analogy between the military and business, as "Washington does nicely playing the company man as nineties hero, an African-American who has learned when to speak up and when to shut up in the white world," adding that "he simmers handsomely but rarely displays the informed rage he showed in *A Soldier's Story* and *Glory*." Which was true, to an extent; but those were utterly different movies, and the comparison was hardly apt.

This wasn't a movie that called for "informed rage." Hunter was a well-educated man. You knew he'd earned his rank and position, and probably had to work twice as hard to get it because he was black. He was degreed, versed in culture high and low. He'd been profiled and highly trained, prepared to deal with extreme situations. That was his job. He knew how to be calm, collected, and how to be a leader, to be in control. And that was how Denzel played him, a thoroughly modern man, aware of his color, but able to discount it under the blue uniform.

Crimson Tide, as Denzel and Hackman played it, was both an intellectual battle, and the new Navy of computers, technology, and science against the old seat-of-the-pants, trusting-your-gut Navy. But unlike Ramsey, Hunter had a center, a life that existed outside the service. He was in touch with a world beyond the sea, and that made him more alive, more rounded than Ramsey could ever hope to be.

Ramsey expected loyalty as his due. Hunter knew he had to earn it, and he was willing to take the steps to do just that. He thought ahead, considered the consequences of his actions. His brain was working every second.

That was what Denzel put across in his portrayal—a man of great intellect, some charm, and a large understanding of the world. Power was relatively new to him, but he was capable of handling it, of not panicking. There probably wasn't another actor in America who could have made those things so implicit in his reading, and made the audience understand Hunter, with just a few gestures and emphases. Nor were there many actors who could have held their own against Hackman when he was at full power.

Entertainment Weekly hit it on the head by writing, "The two actors turn the film into a riveting Oedipal military duel. . . . What holds us is the sight of two superlatively fierce actors working at the top of their game," noting that "Washington makes us register Hunter's wary moral intelligence as a kind of physical force."

Not for nothing were Denzel and Hackman very much the co-stars of this film, both their names together above the titles (with Denzel's notably coming first). Yes, it was entertainment, but what was wrong with that? Most cinema always had been. The real point was that it was excellently done, almost two hours of enthralling acting. That was the payoff, and audiences showed themselves glad of it throughout the summer, regardless of any negatives the critics might have brought up.

Perhaps the sole star billing hadn't gone to Denzel, but that was coming. All too soon . . .

The impetus for Denzel to involve himself in the cyber-thriller *Virtuosity* came not only from the business, but also from home, when his son John David said, "Dad, do something hip instead of those old-man movies."

How could a father turn down a request like that, particularly after he'd been offered the script for this movie, along with a seven million dollar paycheck?

It wasn't meant to be high art (except perhaps high state of the art) or drama—simply good, strong entertainment, a thriller with plenty of special effects.

And that was precisely what landed in the theaters around the country, a movie set just slightly in the future—in 1999, to be exact—with one foot in science fiction, and the other in reality.

Denzel played Parker Barnes, a former policeman who'd once been one of Los Angeles's best cops. But after a terrorist, Matthew Grimes, killed his wife and daughter, Barnes had tracked Grimes down and exacted some very deadly revenge, losing an arm (replaced by a prosthetic device) in the process.

For his trouble in helping stamp out evil, Parker Barnes was now languishing in a prison cell. But there was work waiting for him.

The Law Enforcement Technology Advancement Center (LETAC) used Parker and another prisoner, John Donovan, to test their new virtual criminal, Sid 6.7. Locked into harnesses, their task was to track him down and apprehend him. Unfortunately, the test went awry, and Donovan was killed. Barnes was returned to his cell, where he was to spend the next seventeen years of his life, by way of a fight with a white supremacist. Not too surprisingly, the detached Barnes easily won.

Meanwhile at LETAC, Sid's creator, Dr. Lindenmeyer (Stephen Spinella) convinced a colleague to put the sexy Sheila 3.2 into an android body. However, before the experiment, the chips that were the soul of Sid were substituted, and when the incubation was finished, a killer was on the loose, with the ability to heal himself, even restore limbs, using the silica from glass—and Lindenmeyer had gone into hiding.

The Los Angeles Police Department, none to eager to let the public know the truth, had one option—use Parker Barnes. In the experiments he'd come closer to Sid than anyone else. He was offered a deal—if he caught Sid, he'd receive a free pardon. Anything less, and he'd be returned to jail to finish his sentence. With nothing to lose, he accepted. But before he could hit the road, an implant was put behind his ear, ostensibly to track him.

Teaming up with psychologist Dr. Madison Carter (Kelly Lynch), Barnes went to Lindenmeyer's apartment, where the pair discovered an ugly truth about Sid. He'd been endowed with the personalities of one hundred eighty-three of history's greatest criminals—including Matthew Grimes. Suddenly, for Parker, it became personal.

Sid had immediately gone on a killing spree. He entered a nightclub called The Media Zone and took the patrons hostage, making sure everything was captured on video before beginning his "symphony of destruction." As police responded to the call, they were shot. Except for Barnes. He managed to pump bullets into Sid. Destroying the android was a different matter altogether, however. He escaped, making his getaway in a police cruiser.

Barnes and Madison were in close pursuit, but he finally lost them by jumping off a bridge.

The question was what he'd do next. And that was soon answered. He killed a man in a shopping arcade. Investigating, Barnes saw a television tuned to a wrestling match being held a few blocks away. Sure enough, Sid was there, but he was always one step ahead. Dashing out of the coliseum to a train station, he pulled a hostage in front of him, and dared Barnes to shoot.

Parker did, and the hostage fell to the platform, dead.

As soon as the police arrived, he was arrested, although a quick exam showed that the bullet must have come from Sid's gun. In chains, Barnes was returned to jail.

However, he never arrived. Sid hijacked the truck transporting him, killing the guards and giving Parker the keys to free himself. He wanted a worthy opponent.

And what choice did Parker have? If he stayed he'd be back in prison. If he left, the authorities would assume he'd shot the guards and escaped. But free, he at least had a chance of stopping Sid. So he went, and then called Madison, who placed her own call to the chief of detectives.

What Barnes hadn't known was that his implant contained a small device which, when activated, could kill him. And on the authority of the attorney general, that was about to happen. Until the chief of detectives stopped it.

Sid was about to outdo himself. Hungry for publicity, he took over a live television broadcast, and began to turn it into "Death TV." And the first person to die would be Dr. Carter's daughter, whom he'd kidnapped, and who was now somewhere with a bomb set on a timer.

There wasn't much time. Barnes instructed Carter to have the building manager cut off all the phone lines, depriving Sid of his audience, while he went after the android. On her way, she spotted Lindenmeyer, and took him into custody.

Parker stormed the studio just as the broadcast was curtailed, taking off after Sid, and catching up with him on the roof of the building. After a pitched battle, Barnes was able to throw him down a story, cutting the nonhuman terribly. But he wasn't dead yet, and there was one piece of information Parker needed—the location of the girl.

He almost didn't get it. Sid began to regenerate and held Barnes over a large shard of broken glass. But Parker was finally close enough to kill the simulacrum, reaching into his head to pull out the chip.

The physical danger was gone, but the girl was still somewhere, and neither Carter nor Barnes knew where. All they could do was use Lindenmeyer and return Sid to virtual reality to finish the scenario.

The operation took place under the supervision of the chief of detectives. Once they had their answer, though, the scientist killed the policeman, with Barnes still trapped in the game. It was up to Carter to get him out, and she had to use violence to do it, shooting Lindenmeyer before breaking Parker out of his harness.

They rushed back to the television studio and found the girl tied inside a heating fan vent. The problem was that everything was booby-trapped. It was Barnes against the ghost of Grimes. He'd lost his own wife and daughter to a similar booby trap. Every action he tried to take was blocked. Except one. He managed to set up a loop on an electrical circuit that disabled the bomb. Carefully he removed the girl, and stepped out into the night. Parker Barnes was a free man again, in every way.

It was unfortunate that *Virtuosity* appeared in a season of other cyber-thrillers. Keanu Reeves's supposed techno-blockbuster, *Johnny Mnemonic*, had arrived just a few months earlier. Highly anticipated, it had managed to do only reasonably well at the box office.

Virtuosity, although it had Denzel and some truly spectacular special effects, couldn't even manage that. As director Brett Leonard described it, the movie was supposed to be "a fun, slightly disturbing, balls-to-the-wall roller-coaster ride. It's for the audience that enjoys intensity. Once it starts, it doesn't stop. It's not gory, but where there's evil, there's serious evil, and where there's good, there's serious good; and they definitely slam headlong into each other and create a powerful vibration."

But not a powerful enough vibration to rattle the cinema cash registers. Far more disturbing than the physical violence was the psychological effect of the movie. It played up the violence of intimidation and power. There was some humor, but the darker elements greatly outshadowed it. Sid was seriously evil in more ways than one. What began as an outrageous, almost cartoonish, take on virtual reality and video game technology degenerated into a disturbing nightmare.

It wasn't an easy film to make for anybody involved, but especially Denzel, who thought it "one of the hardest films I've ever done because of the action elements. That was part of the challenge. I've never been in a film where there was so much computer-generated technology. It was an education for me to do this film."

Unfortunately, though, a role like Parker Barnes wasn't one that was ideally suited for Denzel. No matter how well he acted—and he did bring a lot of humanity and warmth to a fairly sterile environment—any performance of his was going to be overwhelmed by the film's technology. Technology was the undoubted star, and his talent—as well as that of the other humans on the screen—was lost among it. No one would have stood a chance. The only person who could shine was Russell Crowe;

as Sid 6.7, he was able to ham and mug as much as he desired. And he did. His character was, literally, larger than life.

None of 1994's cyber-movies proved to be successful. The only one that came close was *The Net*, with Sandra Bullock, which also garnered the best reviews, perhaps because it was the most human of them all. Those with strong science fiction overtones all became lost in the shuffle.

Part of the problem was that they were inevitably going to be compared to the first—and still the best—of the computer effects genre, *Terminator 2*. And beating that was going to be very difficult. Even for someone like Denzel.

Virtuosity wasn't going to be the star vehicle its creators hoped it would be. None of the critics had much good to say about it. *Entertainment Weekly* called it "the latest summer entry in the theater of cyber-inspired cinema," and summed it up as a "nasty, brutish, long training film about what happens when boys spend too much time out of the sunlight, playing with expensive toys." *Maclean's* wrote it off as "a tired reworking of the monster-in-a-box formula," that was, essentially, "about brute force."

But everyone's allowed at least one flop in an otherwise glorious career. And Denzel was, as *Entertainment Weekly* noted, "wasted here," although, *Maclean's* pointed out, he did play the role "with gusto." As a movie made to please his son, it was probably a big success. As something to grab the attention of a paying audience, it failed.

Still, that was hardly the end of the world. There was another film right around the corner, one that would give Denzel more of a chance to act, to be human. Playing a killing machine wasn't his style. Playing a role that had both length and depth definitely was. And that was what was coming up— a return to those basic qualities Denzel projected so well.

TWELVE

Bringing Walter Mosley's first novel, *Devil in a Blue Dress*, to the screen was a daring move. His series of books starring the black private detective Easy Rawlins had sold well, but not to the point where Mosley was a household name. And to make a movie where the main character was a black private eye was treading on thin ice. Would mainstream audiences go to see it?

Carl Franklin, who wrote and directed it, obviously thought so. So did the studio, Jonathan Demme (who signed on as executive producer), and Denzel, who not only agreed to star, but whose production company, Munday Lane, acted as co-producers.

It was the third film he'd shot in a very short space of time, and he knew he'd need a break when he was done. So, before the filming began, he booked a vacation for himself and his family—an African safari. It was something to look forward to, a reward, and a chance to unwind after a long period of intense work.

Ezekiel Rawlins, known as Easy, wasn't really a private detective. He didn't have a license. But in the Los Angeles of 1948, a black man would have found it nearly impossible to become a licensed investigator.

He'd returned from the Army in Europe, and instead of going home to Houston, had settled in L.A. He'd found a job with Champion Aviation, saved his money, and bought a house, a rarity for a black man at the time.

Now, though, he'd lost his job, and he was behind on his mortgage. If anything kept him going, it was the determination not to have his house repossessed. So he pounded the pavement every day, looking for work, and finding nothing.

In Joppy's bar, where he was drinking, the owner introduced him to a white man, Dewitt Allbright, who offered him work. If he were interested, Easy should go to his apartment later.

Although something told him that it wasn't a good idea, Easy went. He was desperate for money. The job seemed small, and paid one hundred dollars, cash. He had to find a white girl, Daphne Monet, who liked to hang around with blacks. She was the girlfriend of Todd Carter, a man running for mayor, and she'd vanished.

That night Easy took himself down to an illegal club he frequented. Running into his friends Dupree and Coretta, he asked them about Daphne. Coretta hinted that she knew her, but wouldn't say more. Finally, late, Easy helped Coretta take a drunk and passed-out Dupree home.

Coretta seduced Easy, teased him with information, and finally, at dawn, gave him an address—for ten dollars. Daphne was staying with a black gangster named Freddy Green. It seemed like he'd done his job, and earned some quick money.

Allbright certainly thought so when they met. He gave Easy another hundred dollars.

But now things began to grow complicated. Arriving home, Easy found two cops waiting for him. They took him downtown, beat him, and began to ask him about Coretta's murder. Someone had killed her, and Easy was the last person she'd been seen with.

Eventually they had to let him go, leaving him to walk home, still bleeding from the head.

On the way a car drew up beside him, and he was invited in. The occupant of the back seat was Terrell, Carter's opponent in the mayoral race. He, too, wanted to know Daphne's whereabouts. It seemed she was a very popular girl. Even for money, Easy couldn't help him.

In the middle of the night, the phone woke a recuperating Easy. It was Daphne (Jennifer Beals).

She was at the Ambassador Hotel, and she wanted to see him.

He made his way there, and sat down with the elusive woman. She and Carter had had a fight, she explained, but now she was ready to go back to him, and she wanted Easy to drive her. But there was one stop she needed to make on the way.

It was in the Hollywood hills, up on Laurel Canyon. She'd given a man a letter to mail, and now she wanted it back. When they arrived at the house, it had been thoroughly searched, and the white man, McGee, was lying dead. Easy knew his face. He'd been trying to get into the club the night before. A pack of Mexican cigarettes was lying beside him, the type favored by the club's bouncer, Junior.

As soon as Daphne saw the body, she ran, took McGee's car, and vanished. Easy was back to square one.

At home, Allbright and his subordinates were waiting. They'd checked out the address Easy had given, and Green hadn't lived there in a year.

Easy told them what he'd discovered since— Coretta's murder, meeting Daphne, finding McGee's body. It seemed to be enough to satisfy Allbright. For now.

Nonetheless, Easy placed a call to his old Houston buddy, Mouse, a man suspected of several killings, and suggested he take a small vacation in L.A.

It was time, he decided, that he pay a visit to the top—to Todd Carter, and find out exactly what was going on. In his best suit, he eventually managed to get to the man, who was astonished that Daphne was even in town; he thought she was hundreds of miles away. He certainly hadn't asked anyone named Allbright to look for her. He offered Easy one thousand dollars to find her. Suddenly everyone wanted to give him money.

The place to start, Easy thought, would be with Frank Green. He knew Green hijacked liquor trucks and sold the bottles down on Central Avenue, so he walked around the liquor stores and bars, acting loud and mentioning Green's name often.

It had an effect. When he got home, Green was waiting, with his knife. Just as it looked as if Easy would lose the fight—and his life—Mouse arrived, with his guns, eager to kill.

A small man, snappily dressed, wearing a bowler hat, Mouse was more or less a psychopath. He shot Green in the shoulder—not exactly what Easy needed.

What he needed even less happened a little later. The two cops who'd beaten him up before showed up on his doorstep, eager to question him about the McGee murder.

Easy cut a deal with them; one more day, and he'd give them all the answers they needed. It put him on the spot, implicated him, but it was better than being dragged downtown and beaten again.

What he needed was the letter Daphne had been seeking at McGee's. It was somewhere. Easy and Mouse went to visit Dupree, Coretta's boyfriend, in the hope he'd know something. As they sat and drank, he mentioned that Coretta had given him a Bible just before she died.

When Dupree passed out, Easy searched his room and found the Bible. Inside was the letter. Except it wasn't a letter, but a series of photos of Terrell with young boys.

Easy went home, leaving Mouse and Dupree to sleep it off. But once again, his homecoming was eventful. Daphne was waiting for him. Easy wanted some answers, some truth from her. And he got them. She loved Carter, but the idea of him marrying her was out of the question—she was half-black. Her mother had been Creole, her father white. Freddie Green was her brother. Carter's family had paid her off to leave him. She'd bought the pictures of Terrell, and was going to use them to see that Carter became mayor. And she knew who'd killed Coretta—it had been Joppy, the bartender.

Before she could go much further, Allbright and his men broke in, and took her. They wanted the photos, and she didn't know where they were. Unable to stop them, Easy watched as they drove her away.

Now he had no choice but to go into action. He

called Mouse, had him come to meet him at Joppy's. Easy went in with a gun, and pulled the man out. Joppy knew Allbright, and knew where he'd have taken Daphne. It was a cabin out near Malibu, a quiet, deserted area.

They drove up, and Easy told Mouse to look after Joppy, but not to shoot him. Then he circled the house, and started shooting.

With the element of surprise, and with Mouse's help, the gangsters were soon dead, and Daphne freed. It was time to go home. But without Joppy. Mouse had strangled him.

Easy delivered Daphne to Carter, even though he knew it could never work out. He waited while they talked, and walked back to the car. Carter paid him, and agreed to keep the police from him.

Easy dropped Daphne off at her brother's apartment. She'd bought the pictures back from him, for seven thousand dollars. Easy was a rich man, even after he'd split the money with Mouse.

When he went back to see her the next week, feeling guilty and thinking of returning the cash to her, she'd gone.

Devil in a Blue Dress was a splendid film in every way. Tautly scripted and directed, superbly acted, it fulfilled every promise of the book. As Richard Schickel wrote in *Time*, it "evokes the spirit of forties film noir more effectively than any movie since *Chinatown*."

And it was reminiscent of *Chinatown* in more than just spirit. Everything brought post-World War II Los Angeles to life, as *Chinatown* had done for the thirties. It also dealt with the corruption of civic officials. Or, as *Rolling Stone* put it, "*Devil* puts a spin on *Chinatown* to provide a black perspective on the layers of corruption that stretch from the streets to the corridors of power."

Calling it a black *Chinatown*, though, would be overly simplistic, for Easy mixed with whites just as much as blacks as the film unfolded. Rather, it was a journey through the different levels of society, and a very powerful one, at that.

It was also, as *Rolling Stone* noted, "whip-smart and sexy," and "smashingly effective at bringing the past alive as entertainment and pointed social history," a point echoed by *Newsweek*, which said, "The evocation of that vanished world is alone worth the price of admission."

Overall, though, the critics remained surprisingly disappointed by the movie. *People* felt it "could turn out to be really special," but "never quite fulfills its early promise. Much of the blame went to director/screenwriter Carl Franklin, who, *Los Angeles* decided, "has been defeated this time around." The film had "one of those wild-goose-chase plots that you're not supposed to care about," as the *Nation* expressed it, but the weight of its complexity ended up tipping it over. "Everything is aces about this lineup's pedigree," *Enter-*

tainment Weekly observed, "But *Devil* never lets loose." Rather, the reviewer observed, Franklin "cools . . . hot spots to a sedate lukewarm."

Still, if critics had a problem with the story, there was little doubt they liked the milieu, and in particular the ending, where Easy walked around his neighborhood, "with a note that's hopeful and elegiac at once, lovely and heartbreaking," said the *Nation*. And, as *Cosmopolitan* pointed out, "This exhilarating montage throbs with hope, vitality, and—best of all—the promise of sequels to come."

Like all great mysteries, it commented on society. Easy was an exception, a black man who owned his own house, and he was determined to keep that anchor in his life. That desire was what dragged him into things, but also what kept him going. His mission was more than finding the truth, but keeping what was his.

There couldn't have been anything better as a vehicle to tip Denzel over the edge into superstardom. With a face that seemed leaner and wearier— perfect for someone who'd been through a war and seen his share of hard times—he *was* Easy, a man with pride and determination, who took his beatings and bounced back a little slower and wiser each time. It also made its point as to the station of blacks in post-World War II society. Even in the more relaxed atmosphere of California, oppression remained. Easy had clawed out a life for himself, but the hold he was allowed to keep on it was tenuous; and still dependent on the white man, who held all the cards. What helped it cross over and appeal to the white audience was the "noir" element of the story. It was Raymond Chandler with an African-American hero, a man every bit as upright and trustworthy as Philip Marlowe. The mystery of the story was universal; indeed, its precursors were in white detective fiction of the thirties and forties.

Denzel could have been born to play this part. Without a doubt, he was masterful at it, taking a character who had already come very much alive in the pages of Walter Mosley's book and rounding off the edges. Just as he had accomplished so often in the past, this wasn't Denzel playing Easy. This was just Easy. Denzel provided nothing more than the flesh and blood vessel for the character. But one thing he couldn't help but add was his natural charisma. He made it believable that people would want to talk to Easy, that a black man could enter the office of a rich white politician and then sit and chat with him. Denzel's performance suspended any disbelief the audience might have had. He easily carried the picture on his shoulders, managing to somehow outdo even his own work in *Malcolm X*, *Glory*, and *Philadelphia*. After this there was no one who could have said he wasn't a true star.

The critics were easily won over by his work. For *Cosmopolitan*, this was the role he had always needed. "The man has charisma to burn, and it is a joy to see him light up the screen . . ." The *Nation* felt that the role of Easy "calls for an actor who has more than star power . . . someone with such an innate sense of dignity that he wouldn't even *think* of swaggering . . . Denzel Washington has always tended to give just that impression of being intact . . . Washington gets to show off a range few other actors can claim." Even *Los Angeles*, no fan of the picture, admitted that Denzel "can hold the screen through sheer grace and decency." *Rolling Stone* was more succinct, calling his portrayal "perfection . . . richly detailed." *Newsweek* deemed him "a subtle actor and natural-born movie star."

People went so far as to say Easy "may turn out to be his signature role," with a performance that was "sure, sharp, and sexy."

Certainly audiences believed him, and believed that the film was good. They kept coming to see it at the multiplexes week after week, making it into a bona fide hit, even if the dollars taken in never quite matched the effusive praise in the full-page ads for the movie.

It was populist entertainment, but it was also more than that. It was an important film. Previously, the only black action heroes shown on film had been Shaft, or others of the "blaxploitation" ilk. Easy was indubitably a real human being, with his own foibles and failings, the first of his kind in the movies. He showed that even just after the war a black man could show the signs of upward mobility and pride and that black life wasn't all jazz, drinking, and petty violence, but could include hard work, respectability, and a yearning to be settled.

And who better to show that side of life than Denzel? He'd consistently been at the forefront of defining blacks in films. And this time, what he'd given us wasn't something that could be called either a black movie or a white movie, but simply a great American film.

CONCLUSION

To call Denzel Washington the most popular black male movie star today would be true, but it would also be somewhat denigrating to him. More accurate would be to call him simply one of the most popular actors on the screen, period.

He's managed to transcend the barrier called race, and that's something we shouldn't forget. As director Carl Franklin said, "Denzel is blessed. He has 'it.' "

He fully deserves, and has worked for, the success he has achieved. No other black actor has achieved so much or come so far in acceptance by mainstream, or white, America. And it's certainly worth looking at just what he had to overcome to do that.

About the only real precedent is Sidney Poitier, who pushed through so many frontiers in the sixties. He was the first African-American to win the Academy Award for Best Actor, in 1963—and still the only one to have won that award—and among the first to be given starring film roles that showed him as the equal of whites. He appealed to both blacks and whites with a handsomeness and innate integrity that guaranteed him female fans of all colors. Poitier was a sex symbol, albeit a mild one.

Nonetheless, the characters he ended up playing tended to be somewhat asexual—Hollywood wasn't yet ready to come to grips with the idea of black people as fully rounded, sexual beings.

In television, and on the stage, there was no shortage of people making their mark, often in a very big way, as actors like Bill Cosby and Charles Dutton became stars. But the big studios seemed to remain a closed book of sorts until the eighties, when actors like Lou Gossett, Jr. and Howard Rollins, Jr. began to appear regularly onscreen.

While breakthroughs were predicted for both of them, their careers stalled. After a bravura performance as the drill sergeant in *An Officer and a Gentleman*, Gossett found himself being cast more and more in "B" movies and action adventures. Rollins, who had been electrifying in *Ragtime*, took the television route, co-starring with Carroll O'Connor in the series *In the Heat of the Night*—taken from the film that had starred Sidney Poitier, and featuring the memorable line of equality—"They call me *Mister* Tibbs."

So why hadn't there been more major black stars? Much of it had to do with the fact that roles which could be star vehicles for blacks weren't being written, or if they were, the studios weren't producing them.

Had Denzel been even ten years older, he might have never been able to emerge from the wealth of black talent. The opportunities would have been much more limited.

Denzel is a child of the time of civil rights and affirmative action, both of which affirmed his identity as an African-American, told him to be proud of it, and to expect the same treatment as everyone else in this country.

While the reality continues to be shamefully different from the theory, there was a definite change in the cultural climate by the time Denzel reached Hollywood. There was a greater openness to films by, for, about, and starring blacks.

Part of that acceptance was linked undoubtedly to financial reasons, and the realization that the black population made up a good percentage of theatergoers, and wanted films they could identify with.

On top of that, those children of the sixties and the seventies were making their way out to the coast. For years their expectations had been raised that they were truly citizens of the country, people whose hopes and dreams were as good as anyone else's. Now it was time for the system to deliver.

Put all of those things together, and suddenly chances finally began to exist in movies for blacks.

When Hattie McDaniel became the first African-American to win an Academy Award (Best Supporting Actress in 1939, for Mammy in *Gone with the Wind*), gossip columnist Louella Parsons had written: "We are beginning to realize that art has no boundaries and that creed, race, or color must not interfere where credit is due."

With the exception of Poitier's Oscar, it would be almost forty years before the film industry took those words to heart. By the late eighties, there were more projects involving black artists than ever before in Hollywood. While it wasn't yet boiling, the pot was heating up, and it was almost inevitable that *someone* would become a star.

Denzel was the right person in the right place at the right time. He had the talent and the desire, both immensely important for success. More than that, though, he had charisma and looks, both valued in films more than acting ability. That mix of handsomeness had been the making of stars since Douglas Fairbanks. It had worked for Poitier, and now it worked for Denzel.

He could have settled for being the top black actor in pictures. That would certainly have been enough. But Denzel's parents had always drummed into him that he should be the best. And those years of education had repeated the phrase "equality." The best meant the best. Period. Not the best black actor or white actor. Just *the best*. There was no need to pigeonhole his talent by color when he had the ability to do it all. Limitations were for people who accepted them. And Denzel didn't. He refused to let himself be fenced in by a color barrier.

That is why he's been able to go from Steve Biko to Bleek Gilliam to Don Pedro to Easy Rawlins. The opportunities existed, and he took them, or he made his own. He parlayed that initial luck, that serendipity, into being one of the true big names in Hollywood. And, though he would probably choose to downplay it, he is, without a doubt, the biggest black name by far. It may have taken him longer than a white actor, but Denzel Washington is a major star, and a major heartthrob.

Certainly he has no shortage of work lined up for the future, movies that once again will have audiences lining up at the box office. *Courage Under Fire* will see him working with Meg Ryan (a proven screen favorite) and Regina Taylor, while *The Preacher's Wife* (a remake of the 1947 Cary Grant comedy *The Bishop's Wife*) pairs him with superstar Whitney Houston, fresh from her success in *Waiting to Exhale*. As if that weren't quite enough to keep him busy for a while, there was talk of him working with Spike Lee again, this time to portray baseball great Jackie Robinson.

The future looks unlimited. Many people, having

finally achieved Denzel's kind of success, would let it go to their heads. But his feet are very firmly on the ground.

"I am where I am by the grace of God," he explained, "but I haven't had to do anything but work hard to get where I am. I didn't get here from partying with the right people or doing anything other than working hard."

Indeed, the only luxury he indulges himself in is cars.

"I got a Porsche. I drive a big Mercedes now, one of those V-12s. I have a Ferrari also."

But what he doesn't add is that, if it hadn't been for his wife Pauletta's encouragement, he'd never have started buying them. He's *earned* his toys.

Denzel is quite possibly also one of the few major stars today to attend church on a regular basis, the West Angeles Church of God in Christ, or to say quite plainly, "God is my hero."

His faith, and the faith of his minister father before him, is a very important part of his makeup. It's deeply rooted in him, and at the heart of everything he does. It's one of the reasons he gives so much back to the community.

His large gift to Nelson Mandela's Children's Fund might have been well publicized, but there have been many others that haven't received attention.

He happily pledged two and a half million dollars toward the construction of his church's new facility (at the same time Earvin "Magic" Johnson promised five million dollars), a rare act of faith in these times, and one that shows that his beliefs are far more than skin deep.

He and Pauletta gave money and time (perhaps a more valuable commodity for someone of his stature) to The Gathering Place, a center for HIV-positive people in South Central Los Angeles. They helped to raise the half a million dollars that kept the facility open until, finally, a lack of funds and community pressure closed it.

Their involvement began when Pauletta asked Dorothy Brown, who was in charge of the women's and children's programs, what could be done. Because of some mix of shame and fear, women simply wouldn't come to the place. Brown offered a few suggestions, and that was all Pauletta needed. She took it from there. Denzel bought the shelter a van, and they began raising money.

Then Denzel himself showed up, volunteering his time to play with the babies and to be a baby-sitter. He sat and talked to the women. And that made all the difference in the world, as Dorothy Brown recalled.

"See, someone who mattered told them *they* mattered. He gave them years. He gave them a reason for living. We think a lot of that brother here."

While filming *Devil in a Blue Dress*, he came across a homeless shelter that needed sewing machines.

Denzel wrote a check, enabling them to buy twenty machines. "To be able to do that is cool," was his comment.

Since 1992 he's also been the national spokesman for the Boys and Girls Clubs of America. When he was young, Denzel spent quite a lot of his free time at the Boys Club in Mt. Vernon, to the point of describing it as "a second home." He never forgot what it gave him, and now he was able to give something back, doing, among other things, public service announcements for the organization, using his influence as a role model to try and put kids on a straight, sane path.

"When you come through the Club, you leave with the realization that you can become a top lawyer, teacher, whatever your heart desires. If you listen to the lessons taught there and apply yourself, you will succeed. I promise you."

Just because Denzel is a firm believer in tithing, giving to charity, and helping those less fortunate doesn't mean he advocates the handout or free ride to everybody. Quite the opposite. Having come up through sheer hard work himself, from an early age, he knows the value of a job, and it's something he wants his own children to have, even though, financially, it's hardly necessary.

Soon, in fact, he plans to put his older son, John David, to work on one of his movies, to "start him at the bottom as a runner, production assistant, and let him go get coffee, learn the whole business."

While that would give the boy a start, Denzel won't force any of his children into a career path in acting.

"... I'm not putting any pressure on them to be anything except decent individuals and hard-working," he told *Ebony*.

And those, perhaps, are the real watchwords to describe Denzel—decent and hardworking. He's become a major celebrity, a personality who can command more money for a film than either Brad Pitt or Keanu Reeves, but he remains a man who carries around taped sermons by his minister and reads *The Daily Word* every morning. Who he is away from the set is completely different from the person we see onscreen. He's an actor, a consummate professional, someone who's served a long apprenticeship, become a journeyman, and has finally achieved stardom through his own talents and abilities.

He's been justifiably honored, one of the winners in the seventh Essence Awards in 1994, and he also received a Career Achievement Award from the American Black Achievement Awards that same year.

Having come so far, and attained so much, it would be easy to think that he would be perfectly content with his level of success, willing to sit back and let the good roles come to him. But that would be to underestimate Denzel. He remains a man who's constantly seeking challenges, new mountains to climb. Apart from his intense period of filming, 1994 also saw him involved with the stage revival of the musical *Carousel* in New York, and guesting with the Alvin Ailey American Dance Theater during its production of *Hymn*.

His production company, Munday Lane (named, incidentally, for the street where he grew up), was one of the producers of *Devil in a Blue Dress*, and Denzel himself was the executive producer of a television special on Hank Aaron that aired on cable station TBS and garnered an Emmy nomination.

It's a different, if connected, avenue for him, and one that holds much potential. But in every phase of his life, Denzel is taking care of the things that need, and that he wants, to be done.

"Everything I want to do, I'm pretty much knocking those things off one at a time."

He's even gone into the restaurant business, as one of the co-owners of the upscale Georgia, a Southern-style place on Los Angeles's famous Melrose Avenue.

There are those who would say he's one of the luckiest men in America. He has a career that's vaulted him into the stratosphere, plenty of money, a very solid family life, the adulation of millions.

And while luck has had something to do with it, at the bottom, at the heart of it all, is talent and work.

Without talent, Denzel wouldn't have made his name in *A Soldier's Play* or *When the Chickens Come*

Home to Roost. Without his God-given ability, he couldn't have gone on from there to *St. Elsewhere* and *Cry Freedom,* or to the critical heights of *Glory* and *Malcolm X.*

There are stars who are made. As actors they may not be much, but they have the look, and they photograph well. They might flash across the sky, famous for a short while. But the public can only be fooled by a pretty face for so long. For a career to last, it has to have some substance. And Denzel's work is full of substance. He's been involved with more quality films than almost any actor of his generation. It doesn't matter whether they were "black" films like *Mo' Better Blues* or movies for mass consumption, like *Crimson Tide.* His name in the cast is a virtual guarantee of quality.

The talent that's brought him this far has also been backed up by plenty of hard work, years and years of it. Every time he accepts a role, he pours himself into it wholeheartedly. He researches his characters extensively, discovers what makes them tick, and becomes them. He *works* at it. He began doing it that way because that was how the very best did it. And Denzel wanted his name up there with theirs.

"When I looked at the actors I liked, and I did my research, I said, Well, that's what they do. That's what Meryl does. That's what Dustin does. That's what Al Pacino does. Sidney Poitier. De

Niro. I watched *Mean Streets* three thousand times."

The people he looked up to were all stars. But they all had become stars through their acting ability. Not for their faces or their personalities. Rather, they were the ones who could totally submerge themselves in their roles, make themselves disappear, so the person viewers saw on the screen was not De Niro or Streep, but Travis Bickle or Sophie. They had an almost magical quality he wanted to emulate, and that he's more than succeeded in doing. In fact, by playing roles originally written for white actors—Billings in *Power*, Joe Miller, Don Pedro, Gray Grantham—and made the parts utterly his, he's perhaps gone even further than they have. And he's certainly added his name to a very select list of screen idols who are also great actors. Like Hoffman and Pacino and the others, Denzel remakes himself every time he appears in front of the camera, an empty vessel that fills up with a new character. His stardom has been earned, not handed to him by publicists and magazines.

And these days, at this point in Denzel's career, you can no longer say it's a black thing. Or a white thing. It's a human thing.

The fact that *Devil in a Blue Dress* is dominated by black characters, that such a story can attract a mass audience, is testament to the way many of the attitudes in America have changed. It is also a testament to the drawing power of Denzel Washington.

The movie's success, both popular and critical, shows just how big a star he's become.

"I bring myself to any part," he said. "And I'll bring my experiences and voice my opinions."

Obviously, after his time in the business, seeing it from the bottom as well as the top, those experiences and opinions are valuable. He's learned his lessons well. He understands how blacks are seen—or often not seen; he can still go into a movie theater, and be unrecognized by white crowds. He knows the distance we still have to go.

Even today he can be the victim of racism, sometimes overt, like not being able to get that cab in New York, at other times, more insidious, such as being on an elevator with a white woman and watching her clutch her purse in fear.

"I want to take my wallet out and just tap her on her head and say, 'Honey, don't worry about it. I think I've got a couple of more dollars than you.' "

It's perhaps easy for him to laugh about it. That helps take away the pain. But Denzel understands that if it can happen to him, one of the most successful black people in America, then for the average African-American it can only be much, much worse. And it happens every day.

He's never been afraid of saying what he feels about it. He complained about the movie *Pulp Fiction*, one of the major successes of the nineties, because it repeatedly used the word "nigger." Equally, he'll criticize an upcoming generation of black filmmakers for endlessly recycling life in the 'hood stories.

"That story's been told," he explained in *Time*. "If someone has something to spill from their heart, God bless 'em, they should . . . but if someone's just saying, 'Oh, I'm gonna keep doing this 'cause it makes money,' I'll be the first person in line to punch that person in the head."

But Denzel knows about it coming from the heart. That's where his characterizations originate. His research is meticulous, but more than anything else, the way he convinces is in his *feel* of the role.

"I have faith. I jump in the water. I don't try to figure it all out. I do better with being the best that I can be."

So what, apart from as much work as he can handle, does the future hold for Denzel Washington?

"Hopefully evolving, growing, trying to get better," he said. "That's what I would say. I try to be ego-less, if there is such a thing. I try to stay humble and hungry . . . just hungry to be good at my job. A little hunger is good for you."

It keeps his feet firmly planted on the ground, and it's unlikely that anything can happen now to let him drift away. He's seen the adulation, and kept himself at one remove from it. His family— his rock, his anchor—is there, around him, to make sure things can never get far out of hand.

He works, and works hard, at what he does. And what he does, Denzel does very well. In its essence, that's the way he lives. His mother once told him, "Keep it simple. Life is not that complicated," and it's a philosophy he's tried to live by. Hard work creates its own rewards.

"I think if I wanted something put on my tombstone, I'd put, 'Hard work is good enough.'"

But it'll be many years, and many, many films before that happens. Denzel Washington has a long time to work hard yet.

AN UP-CLOSE LOOK AT THE ACTOR WHO HAS REINVENTED THE "LATIN LOVER" FOR A WHOLE NEW GENERATION!

When Antonio Banderas exploded off movie screens as the fiery symbol of Spain's new rebel spirit, all the world took notice. Then he broke the language barrier with *The Mambo Kings*, and shattered all Hollywood conventions as Tom Hanks' gay lover in *Philadelphia*. Celebrity biographer Kathleen Tracy shows us what makes Antonio tick...personally, professionally, and romantically.

ANTONIO BANDERAS

KATHLEEN TRACY